ECONOMIC INCLUSIVISM. Neo-Capitalism/An Anthology.
Inclusive pro-market solutions to our social problems

By

Jim Green

DEDICATED TO:

All who seek to make the world a better place....

ISBN-13: 978-1481278430

ISBN-10: 1481278436

PROLOGUE

As I write--the Sandy Hook Elementary School shooting is unfolding—at present the scene is chaotic—and the information about what happened is equally as chaotic—the scene and scenario have become all too familiar in America....

And the objective of Economic Inclusivism [hereafter EI] is, in part, to address this type of insanity, in America—but first we must get honest about America—about "American Exceptionalism"—in the pejorative sense--

For example, we have a racist component in America that has never accepted President Obama as being a legitimate president—solely because he is black—[the R in Republican in the South, stands for "Racist"]--and raised, here, because we are not honest about this—and if we are ever going to solve our problems in America—First, we have to start getting honest about them! [more on this later]

We are in the throes of enormous socioeconomic change. With the advent of the new world market economy--Globalization, and the proliferation of new technology/automation—the world has changed, our solutions haven't, and the result has been a disaster!

Over the past 60 years our solution to our shifting and shrinking world has been to create a Welfare State. Almost everyone agrees today, however, that this interim step is no longer viable--and indeed, is inhumane.

Inexplicably, some persons feel that our solution is to "go back" to an earlier time--and provincial wisdom is to leave the solution in the hands of fate and the whims of the "free market". The reality is, however, that the "free market" has never been able to provide productive employment for everyone--in spite of the _myth_ to the contrary. The mere existence of our Welfare State stands as solid evidence to the erroneous nature of this myth—

Further, it would be impossible to have a 7.8% unemployment rate—[12 million Americans still unemployed]--and suggest that we are on the right path to solve this problem—the sheer numbers are the proof--

Also, and for absolute clarity, I am a capitalist—EI is a Pro-Market solution—and contrary to their propaganda, the Republican agenda is _harmful_ to the market—the solutions proposed by the Republicans in Congress are _anti-capitalism_--and we are long over-due in confronting them on their _fraud_--[pandering to the *greed* of the 1% is the One and Only program of the Republican party, today—and their claim that this is pro-market--is a LIE]¹

Further, by the year 2015 [today], it is predicted that over 50% of the world's population will live in mega-cities, each with many millions in population.

For instance, Tokyo has population of 33.8 million, today, New York City and Mexico City are tied at 19 million—the list goes on-- "In 1950, there was only one city with a population of more than 10 million, New York. In 2015 there will be 21, and the number of urban areas with populations between five and ten million will shoot from 7 to 37." (National Geographic, November, 2002).

The following letter of Thanksgiving Day, 2012, hopefully will frame the issues raised, here--

President Obama/Council of Economic Advisers:

RE: LAYING the FOUNDATION for RECOVERY & GROWTH

President Obama had a weapon in addressing our economic meltdown in 2008, in America—not available to FDR during the Great Depression:

And this was the hundreds of billions from Military Retirement and Social Security Insurance percolating up through our economy—

In short, were it not for these moneys we would not be talking about having narrowly averted another Great Depression—we would be buried in one!

Also, this model is a "win-win"—it addresses a critical social need, as well as benefits the economy i.e., the market—and yet the Republicans want to tamper with this vibrant social benefit in their short-sighted agenda to pander to the _greed_ of the 1%--it is their One and Only program!

In short, this model is a "pro-market" concept—and least understood. An _indispensable_ component to the proper functioning of the market going forward in the 21st Century—

The market thrives when we have a robust, employed, consuming workforce—but given the proliferating volatile nature of the market [the obsolete cycle is getting shorter and shorter], _the market is no longer capable of producing the jobs necessary to its viability_—and it is essential that we address this void with public sector jobs—_on behalf of the market_!

The Buffer Stock Employment Model introduced at the University of Chicago in 1998, by Dr. William Mitchell, signaled a solution to this economic dilemma facing a modern market economy. Fix the market and this will fix our unemployment crisis vs fix unemployment and this will in turn fix the market—

"Conventional Wisdom", to date, has exclusively taken the former path—and the result has been a disaster—and in spite of a 7.8% unemployment rate—we still have 12 million jobless Americans, a sluggish recovery—and a CBO projection of 5 years just to get back to 5.5%--with unemployment benefits long since expired!

Proposed, here, is The Neighbor-To-Neighbor Job Creation Act. A federally mandated mutual insurance, owned by our employed, to provide a fund to hire/train our unemployed. For a modest policy cost of 4% of salary we can reduce our unemployment to 3%, within a year of passage, and as "authorized" under Public Law 15 USC § 3101. The lone legislation in Washington, at present, relevant to the above is HR 870 [currently in Committee].

See also, "OUR GREED AND IGNORANCE" on Amazon/Kindle; www.Inclusivism.org .

Jim Green, Democrat candidate for Congress, 2000

This is my 9th book—it should have been my first—the proposed changes outlined in EI are the roots for 6 of the 8 books published—and included here as an anthology—hopefully with deleted redundancy—albeit, some of the points bear repeating--

We did not arrive at this cross-road in our history in a vacuum, and in an effort to counter our current dangerous direction and agenda, I have looked to root causes and outlined the following alternative bifurcated solution for economic/prison reforms (which in this context bear a symbiotic relationship to each other).

We do not need to turn America into a police state, with severely diminished civil liberties (both part of the plan and propaganda by the extreme right) but we must make certain systemic changes, i.e., we do have a choice.

Specifically, we need to take certain legislative and constitutional reform action so that we can intelligently address the social chaos and apathy which has been caused by the colliding forces of globalization and automation/technology on our social institutions.

These forces, while offering enormous social benefits, have also created a whole new set of social problems, including disintegration of the family, and the proliferation of violence in our schools, churches and workplaces; and thus call for a whole new set of social solutions.

Our response as individuals to the negative side effects of globalization and automation/technology has resulted in an explosion in the sale of home security devices, as we barricade ourselves in our homes.

Before WW II, it was not uncommon for families to leave their homes unlocked when they went away on vacation.

On a governmental level, over the past 50 years plus, we have chosen Band-Aid programs to counter these adverse effects, over systemic change, and built the largest prison system in the world.

Indeed, every dollar we waste in our insatiable need to incarcerate persons, is a dollar that is deducted from educating our youth, given our equally insatiable demand for lower taxes.

The problem, it seems, is one of twisted priorities where we spend billions in tax dollars annually to correct problems we ourselves have created by inept Band-Aid programs/policies!

And the War against Iraq is a textbook example of our twisted priorities where we almost bankrupted America with a problem we should never have created in the first place!

The solution proposed, here, is devoid of an ideological agenda and the sole criteria has been to find practical solutions, which, when applied in concert, will both preserve our freedoms under the Bill of Rights, and create a "safe and sane" environment in which to live and raise our children in our 21st Century economy.

Indeed, it is asserted that the systemic changes proposed, here, provide the only _viable_ means we have [via this mind-set] by which to preserve the Bill of Rights, and reverse our current oppressive police state solutions.

All other paths lead to further diminution of our individual civil liberties. My background for this proposed solution includes over 20 years employment in the American criminal justice system, as a probation officer and chief probation officer, and I was a candidate for Congress in the 2000 election. I have titled this seven-point program for economic/social reform www.Inclusivism.org .

ECONOMIC INCLUSIVISM: A 21st Century Solution

[Social/Prison Reforms]

1) We need to re-classify all crime in the future as "violent" or "non-violent", and discard the archaic terms "felony" and "misdemeanor". The word felony has been implanted in the public's mind to mean "armed and dangerous"....and yet over 70% of our prison inmates (all felons)are in prison for non-violent offenses....as a result, the term "felony" is distracting us from addressing the real problem....the violent offender.

2) We need a much greater use of "Shock" Incarceration (A sentencing alternative I authored in the 1960's); a greater use of fines and probation (both civil and criminal), in lieu of incarceration, and an expanded menu of sentencing alternatives. [We have 5% of the world's population, and 25% of all prison inmates on earth, in our prisons! If we had the same proportion of inmates to general population as the rest of the civilized world, we would have 400,000 persons incarcerated, not over 2,000,000, as we do at present! And yet our PR is that we are the most free country in the world? We daily turn non-violent persons into violent career criminals, with over 99% released back into society, making life in America MORE dangerous, not less! Prison should be a last resort, not first.]

3) We need the creation of Federal Regional Diagnostic and Treatment Centers, for the diagnosis and treatment of the violent offender. We have learned a great deal about violent behavior in recent years (see www.brainplace.com), and yet we do not have a

cohesive or concerted national program or policy in America for dealing with this national epidemic and disgrace. The sheer numbers of homicides by handguns, alone, tells the whole story, Canada 151, Australia 57, Germany 373, Japan 19, England and Wales 54, the United States 11,789 [numbers which remain static, year after year]1 And, when we add in all deaths by guns, including the fact that 9 children are killed by guns everyday in America, our gun violence escalates to a staggering 28,6631 Also, we need to allow for voluntary admissions to these Centers, to prevent juvenile and family violence. It is essential that we seek out "problem-solving", not "punishment" oriented solutions, which actually exacerbate crime. [As a brief addendum, here—this was originally written 15 years ago—not as the horrible disaster unfolds at Sandy Hook]--

4) We need to pick-up the lead taken by England, in treating drug addiction as a "medical" rather than a "criminal" problem, so that we can EFFECTIVELY curb drug-related crime, and keep drugs out of the hands of our youth. To demonstrate how specious our thinking has become in this area, alcohol and tobacco kill ten of thousands of persons annually, and yet these drugs are not classified as "dangerous". The tiny handful of persons with "addictive personalities" has totally shaped our drug policies while "addiction", in all of its forms, can only EFFECTIVELY be treated with a medical solution. We have wasted billions on interdiction, and yet, youth drug abuse is actually increasing.

[Economic Reforms]

5) To address our insidious practice of "exclusion", Congress must enforce a citizen's legal right to work, as enacted by Congress in "The Full Employment Act of 1946", and reaffirmed in 1978--and as outlined in the Democratic National Platform position asserting "Opportunity to every American". The right to work and be a productive member of one's society is also a human right. Accordingly, we must ratify the following constitutional amendment. "Work shall hereafter be the legal right of every citizen, and Congress shall, except for retirement/disability programs under federal jurisdiction, make no laws which will abridge the right of any citizen of legal age, to work and be a productive citizen." [Our lapse in enlightenment regarding this urgently needed systemic change -- believed by the ignorant and uninformed to be "socialism or communism" – and combined with some really peculiar notions about guns, is the cause for almost all violent crime in America]. Outlined in more detail, herein--

6) To ensure enforcement/fund this legal right, Congress would create a privately owned, federally mandated, Mutual Insurance plan, owned by our employed to provide a fund to hire/train our unemployed. Work could include. Child care for low income working families, building a high-speed rail system, the urgent

need outlined by the NEA for School Modernization, the creation of Federal Regional Diagnostic and Treatment Centers for the diagnosis and treatment of the violent offender, repairing our rotting infrastructure [the list of social benefits is endless]. As owners of this plan, each worker could vote on proposed national projects and dividends would be paid annually from unused funds. A projected policy cost of 4% of salary would reduce our unemployment to 3%, within a year of passage, and as "authorized" under Public Law . [Like Social Security and military retirement moneys, Economic Inclusivism would *strengthen*, not weaken the business community....these steps are necessary to preserve, not harm capitalism in a rapidly changing economy....and prevent our further movement down the erroneous path towards communism or towards the other extreme, fascism (our current movement), both of which require a dictator, and the wholesale loss of our civil liberties, to hold the government in place.]

7) Since this program of "inclusion" would address 95% of our social ills (crime, welfare, drugs, etc., and exacerbated in many cases by inept Band-Aid programs), the federal budget could be greatly reduced and our current Federal Income Tax would be replaced with a National Sales Tax, value-added tax, a national lottery, or some combination of taxes other than our current Federal Income Tax. We currently spend $14 billion annually for the Internal Revenue Service, and corporations and individuals

spend trillions trying to get around the Tax Code, all of which is passed on to us, the consumer, in the higher cost of consumer goods.

A few closing comments—As Oscar Wilde averred "The only truly worthless opinion is an unbiased one"—so bias, agreed—but always in the interest in getting at the larger goal—the truth....Incidentally, I published my first book on my 78th birthday—and have published a book a month since--this is my ninth [and my last—only few are included, here—2 are in a different genre]—and not that I write that fast, or well—the materials were all there for the better part of the past 30 years, give or take, gathering dust—it was just a matter of pulling them together in some order—also, don't believe any book should be over 60 pages, plus/minus—[this book is the exception, of course] i.e., can be read in the crapper--two hours, max--lol—but it seems best summed up by a very astute observer [wish I could recall their name to give credit] but re the long delay in publishing, Persons who write do so because they have no choice [it is a compulsion, an addiction..]—they become an "author", however, when people start reading what they have written....

Finally, a note to the reader—the papers and letters are not in sequence, and there is some redundancy [please look for the nuggets...Thx--lol]—also, if you are a "typo-wonk"—are more concerned with sentence structure, etc., than content—you probably won't like my writing—and you will find a wayward capital letter, here and there, and appearing out of place and used for emphasis—I chalk up to editorial license and tongue-in-cheek, self-effacing humor—so apologies, here—[I seriously support. Take what you do seriously, but never yourself....]....

Just look for content, please....THX

ANTHOLOGY I

OUR GREED & IGNORANCE:

Poses A Far Greater Danger To America, Than Terrorism

Where is the truth in America? If America fails it will have two
parents: GREED AND IGNORANCE—Greed on the part of the 1%,
and Ignorance by those in the 99% who are in the "bubble", and
who are unwilling, or unable to inform themselves, and thus vote
Republican—a truth in America, today—and Republican
Conservative, and 30-year Congressional insider, Mike Lofgren,
nailed it regarding the Republican Party, today--with the
"Republicans went crazy"....

For starters--Paul Ryan is not a decent person. Why does our
media not tell the truth regarding this person—the unvarnished
truth? Like his mendacity at the Republican Convention—telling
one lie after another--and how can he claim to be a champion of
deficit reduction—and rail against President Obama—when he
voted to add $5 trillion to our deficit under Bush!

What a hypocrite! And the "Nuns On A Bus" nailed him for his
anti-Christian views—Ryan claims to be a "Christian"—if one is
not following he teachings of Christ—they are NOT a Christian—
[and this net can be drawn over the entire Republican agenda]--
so why does our media not confront them on their views?

Ryan is only one of many in the current Republican line-up, however—And, where is the Republican apology? Apparently aware of the problem, and that the question would be asked, Romney jumped out ahead with his book "No Apology"—

When, in fact, neither Romney nor any Republican for national office should be permitted to say even one word in this election—until they first profusely apologize to the American people for the damage Republicans have done to America, when they have been in the White House, over the past 32 years!

It is the decent thing to do! A decent person would have done this long ago—during the Republican debates! And, where was our media calling for this apology during the debates? It is our only assurance that the Republicans will never again put America in peril, if elected!

For instance, our deficit was $60 billion in 1980—and like a juvenile delinquent with their parent's stolen credit card—the Republicans ran up debt on the American people to a staggering criminal $10 trillion by 2008—and it has cost an additional $5 trillion, mostly in corporate welfare, to bring this runaway train under control—with some economists calling for even more to correct the damage done as a result of the Republicans being in the White House!

"Stupid" is crass, street language—to be used sparingly—and used because it is the best word in the interest of getting at the Truth---also, the reference, here, is not regarding individual IQ, but rather, for instance, their claim to be the pro-market "free enterprise" party—when more businesses have failed as a direct result of Republican policies than at any other time in American history!

The agenda of the Republican Party, today, is "Greed For The Sake Of Greed" --Period, they have no other agenda—[no investment in the betterment of America]—and the sole objective of the Republicans in Congress is to pander to this GREED—it is "stupid" because it is anti-capitalism—this posture is anti-the business community—and our business failures are the proof! The Republican agenda, today, is solely to make the already rich, richer--

Ryan and company want to do away with Social Security and Medicare—because it doesn't "pander to the greed of the Republican's wealthiest contributors" [to eliminate their paying taxes]—and Romney wants to cut their taxes even further!

There is a bright line between cut taxes for the 1%, and eliminate America's social safety net—and it is driven solely by GREED!

Ryan, et al are stupid because of their indifference to a weapon available to President Obama, not available to FDR—specifically, if it were not for our Social Security and military retirement moneys percolating up through our economy—we would not be talking about having narrowly averted another Great Depression—we would be buried in one!

Social Security—our social insurance--is a Pro-Market solution!

In short, it is stupid for the Republicans to undermine these social programs—because even our most greedy will be injured in the long run!

We can't siphon America's wealth away from the consuming middle [and particularly for the shallow objective of greed, just for the sake of greed]—without sending our economy into meltdown!

Reaganomics has a shelf-life of about 7 years before the economy collapses—as we learned in 1987 [when the stock market lost a quarter of its value in one day], and again 2008—and the American taxpayers had to rush in, in both cases, with trillions of dollars to prevent the imminent collapse of our economy!

Another annoying element in the Republican propaganda blather, today, is the nonsense that Reagan was a "great" president—

Reagan wasn't even mediocre—relegating America to the 8th Century when we had kings and serfs--isn't "revolutionary"—it is a rejection of modernity—and history will record that Reagan was the worst president in American history, until Bush II bumped him out of last place!

So why is our media allowing the Republicans to get away with this BS?

The national Republicans Party, today, has traded GOP for NDP [Not Decent People]—Rove, Limbaugh, Ryan, Glenn Beck [the list is almost endless] in this strata—and it is time we started fessing up to the truth in America!

In sum, the agenda of the national Republican Party, today, is based on the exact same tactic as Hitler's "Big Lie"—and it is equally as deceptive and despicable—no decent person would advocate what Romney and Ryan are advocating!

And it is directed at our ignorant and those suffering from feelings of low self-esteem—those who are awash in magical and wishful thinking, theological terrorism, and those who are suffering from amnesia [What R & R are advocating has a track record—IT DOESN'T WORK]! And their pitch is to cover up their real agenda. To make our already rich, richer—Period, the national Republican Party stands for NOTHING else!

The following letters expand on the above—and as Oscar Wilde averred "The only truly worthless opinion is an unbiased one"—so bias, agreed—but always in the interest in getting at the larger goal—the truth....

Finally, a note to the reader—the letters are mostly letters to the editor, relative at the time--not in sequence, and some redundancy [please look for the nuggets....]—also, if you are a "typo-wonk"—are more concerned with sentence structure, etc., than content—you probably won't like my writing—and a wayward capital letter, here and there, and appearing out of place and used for emphasis—editorial license—so apologies, here—

Just look for content, please....THX

CHAPTER ONE

The More We Change, The More We Stay The Same....

Editor/NY Times:

A Republican candidate for president said "On next January 20, there will begin in Washington, the biggest unraveling, unsnarling, untangling operation in our nation's history."

But before Republican ideologues say "right on" regarding President Obama—this was from an archive speech by Republican candidate Tom Dewey, and directed at President Truman, in 1948.

Will politics never change? Given the political rhetoric you would think President Truman couldn't even tie his own shoes—albeit, he had ended WWII [while President Obama has rescued America from another Great Depression].

And other parallels between these two elections are even more striking.

For instance, Truman was outraged by what he called a "Do nothing Congress"—and he went on the warn the electorate that

"The country cannot afford another Republican Congress." Are we in an echo chamber, here?

The most startling parallel, however, is when Truman said of the Republican Congress on a stump speech "It is a sad tale of the sell out of the American people to these gluttons of privilege—these cold men who skim the cream from our natural resources to satisfy their own greed."

This could have been said yesterday, and yet, it was said by President Truman 64 years ago!

Finally, President Truman offered some words of wisdom to the American electorate on the danger or returning our government back to the Republicans [as true today, as then] "I'm just waking you up to the fact that this is YOUR fight—and YOU are going to be the loser [if you return the White House back to the Republicans]."

And, as every student of History knows, and in spite of the inexcusable headline error by the Chicago Tribune "DEWEY DEFEATS TRUMAN"—President Truman won.

Jim Green, Democrat candidate for Congress, 2000

CHAPTER TWO

The Truth About Healthcare,

Editor/NY Times,

It is amazing the people, mostly Tea Party, railing against the Patient Protection and Affordable Care Act (PPACA), signed into law by President Obama, on March 23, 2010.

The truth is, the only persons in the rank and file who are railing against PPACA, are those who don't know what we have now...

Don't they know they have been duped? Made suckers of by the "profit-takers" [who don't even so much as put a Band-Aid on a patient]--who skim tens of billion of dollars out of our healthcare system in America—purely in the name of GREED!

Our healthcare system in America is an $800 billion a year industry [17% of our GDP], and the "profit-takers" claim an obscene 30% [almost a third] in "administrative costs"—when those costs are only 5-7% in every other major country in the world! Do the math—It is unlawful to make a "profit" from people's healthcare, in every country except America!

And tens of millions of the "profit" they take out of our healthcare system is used for propaganda ads to make suckers out of the Tea Party, etc—

Ever notice how they throw around the word "Freedom"—they are not talking about OUR freedom—us, the American people—they are talking about THEIR freedom to go on making a pot of gold off of the American people!

And it makes you wonder how many of those protesting in DC, many paid by the "profit-takers" to be there—are not protesting the requirement that everyone who drives must have liability insurance? It is the same principle—and it also drives down the cost---After all, this is a Republican law in Massachusetts—that is, before it became "socialism"-----

The truth is, we pay twice as much for healthcare in America as every other major industrial country—and yet, we are 37th in the world in quality of care, according the World Health Organization—we have the highest infant mortality rate in the world, and overall mortality ranked along side some Third World countries—

And solely because we have a few siphoning billions out of our "for profit" healthcare system—for their personal GREED [hint, not one dime goes to the healthcare of anyone]!

It should be no surprise, then, that they have spent tens of millions in propaganda ads to trick the Tea Party, and other uninformed Americans about PPACA. [What a double-cross, using OUR money to rip us off]!

And, also it should be no surprise that the Republican candidates for president support this rip-off of the American people—because they don't represent us, folks—their ONE AND ONLY program is to pander to the GREED of their wealthiest contributors—PERIOD! They have no other program!

Finally, a few myths need to be exploded—There is NO 'free" healthcare—England, or elsewhere--never has been, never will be—Also, insurance, is insurance—whether car, house or health—WE take it out, and pool our money to share the costs—for OUR protection, if fate taps us on the shoulder—

And yet, at present, 44,000 Americans die every year, solely, because of the excessive costs of health insurance [and so the "profit-takers" can get their piece of the action]—And the biggest myth—no one responsible is saying that medical professionals should not be compensated for their years of training—a GP in England earns on average $200,000—but no one wants a system, including doctors, where persons enter the medical field as a means to get rich, rather than treat the ill.

Jim Green, Democrat candidate for Congress, 2000

www.Inclusivism.org

CHAPTER THREE

THE HISTORY OF HOW WE GOT WHERE WE ARE.

In the mid-1970's, the colliding forces of automation, technology, globalization, etc., reached a critical mass, resulting in ubiquitous unemployment in all of the OECD countries, and has left their leaders conflicted, ever since, regarding the displaced employee— Eurozone unemployment is still in double digits, with Spain at 22.9%, and with high youth unemployment a major factor in Arab Spring.

In the U.S., we took a pro-active role in addressing, and as a direct response to this economic shift—and in 1978 President Carter signed into law 15 USC § 3101--which *authorizes* the creation of a *reservoir of public employment* at any time our unemployment in America exceeds *3%*.

The following year, in 1979, however, and in a panic over Humphrey-Hawkins—our ultra-conservative foundations, and desperate to preserve the *market only* job creation concept, embraced a flawed paper by an obscure MIT student, David L. Birch *The Job Generation Process*; and [with lots of cash] gave his paper biblical importance, and every president since has cited his finding as gospel.

Birch's paper concluded that "small businesses" were the greatest generator of new jobs—problem is, for the purposes of policy-making—it is BS. In a study at Harvard University in 2010, "The Myth of Small Business Job Creation" The research shows "no systematic relationship between firm size and growth." And that small businesses can actually detract from job growth—nevertheless, it is still the Republican One and Only job creation solution!

And in spite of this Washington struggles, still, to make this antiquated and unworkable notion, work--that it is only the market that can create jobs—the world has changed, our solutions haven't, and the result has been a disaster, politically as well as otherwise!

It would be impossible to still have 8.3% unemployment if we were on the right path [the result is the proof]—and among other problems with this concept--if the market fails, the unemployed are out of luck [It is the reason Romeny's job creation solution is a farce!].

Further, unemployment is a "social" problem we are seeking to address with a highly unstable, incompatible entity: The Market --That is, the last place we should look for a reliable solution to our unemployment crisis is The Market....

And, what apparently isn't clear going forward in the 21st Century, is that an expanding and contracting public workforce is an INDISPENSABLE component to the correct functioning of a modern market economy—i.e., The Humphrey-Hawkins Full Employment Act was dead-on correct in 1978—and provided a "win-win" solution for America--

The market thrives when we have a robust, employed, consuming workforce, and it is essential to consumer confidence—and overlooked is that HR 870 [currently in Committee], and the proposed "Neighbor-To-Neighbor Job Creation Act" [hereafter NTN] See: www.Inclusivism.org [both authorized under Humphrey-Hawkins], are deficit-neutral--Pro-Market "win-win" solutions. The American people win, and capitalism wins—

CHAPTER FOUR

Editor/NY Times

There will be a lot of "buyer's remorse" on the part of rank and file Republicans—who voted for Romney/Ryan—if they should actually win—

They will be like the guy who woke up from a serious hangover and found out he had thrown the family cat through the neighbor's window [an old Shelley Berman joke]—

Most of the rank and file I have talked to are so blindly zealous in their vote "against" President Obama—[some based on racism]--they don't have a clue what Romney/Ryan has in store for them.

Specifically, to pick up right where Bush II left off—and we all know how that turned out! Been there—did that—it is called "Supply-Side" or "Reaganomics"—IT DOESN'T WORK! IT IS WHAT CAUSED THE GREAT RECESSION IN 2008!

The national Republican Party has but a single agenda—TO PANDER TO THE GREED OF THEIR WEALTHIEST CONTRIBUTORS! Period! That's it—and rather than investing in the betterment of America, they hide their wealth in secret bank accounts to avoid investing in America--!

Further, we can't siphon America's wealth away from the consuming middle, and give it to the already wealthy, without sending our economy into a tailspin!

"Supply-Side" has a shelf-life of about 7 years before the false premise upon which it is based starts caving in on itself—as we learned in our economic collapse in 1987 and again in 2008 [and getting worse each salvo from this corrupt scheme]—and it has cost the American taxpayers trillions of dollars to put a floor under our economy, in the inevitable meltdown!

President Obama had the grim task, from his first day in office, of saving America from another Great Depression, in 2009—

And the Republican propaganda machine has the gall to snow the rank and file with the false blather [flat out lie] that Obama was a "tax and spend" liberal—Obama is a moderate CONSERVATIVE! And if McCain had been elected he would have taken the exact same steps—the choice was "Stimulus" or an ultra-severe Depression—Period! We were losing 700,000 jobs a month!

Finally, the starting point in our political discussion in this election—MUST begin with a Republican apology as assurance to the American people they will not return to the same failed policies that almost sunk America!

So what rank and file Republicans should be asking, now, is where is the Romney/Ryan profuse apology to the American people for the damage Republican policies have done to America?

Jim Green, Democrat candidate for Congress, 2000 See also: My Letters To President Obama, on Amazon/Kindle

CHAPTER FIVE

Editor/NY Times [re Republican debates].

Has anyone noticed that the Republican candidates for president are selling themselves—NOT on the basis of real solutions, but rather because they are the candidate who can "beat Obama"—

It is a goal that is consummate proof that "winning" trumps what is in the best economic interest of the voter—and no one would vote against their own pocketbook, would they?

Indeed, talk about bad ideas regarding their "solutions"—every Republican candidate wants to return America to the same policies that drove our economy into a ditch in the first place!

To wit, Cut taxes for the 1%, they will build factories with the extra cash—everyone will have a job in the corporation—and we will all live happily ever after—

Yes folks, it's a fairy tale!

In fact, with the extra cash the 1% bought an extra yacht, or more trips to Europe—and by siphoning America's wealth out of the hands of the consuming middle, and into their hands—our economy went into meltdown—TWICE—in 1987 & 2008—

So where was the Tea Party regarding the "stimulus" spending in 1987? Where was their hue and cry that Reagan was a "tax and spend liberal" when he used the exact same economic tool to put a floor under our collapsing economy in 1987?

Indeed, Supply-Side has a shelf-life of about 7 years before the economy goes into meltdown—and it has taken trillions of dollars added to our deficit—IN BOTH OF THESE YEARS—to clean up the mess!

Supply-Side is the major reason America has a $15 trillion deficit—our deficit was only $60 billion in 1980—the government cannot cut off its revenue so it can give a big fat paycheck to the 1%--and add the shortfall in revenue to our deficit for our grandchildren to pay—WITHOUT DRIVING AMERICA INTO MASSIVE DEBT!

Return to this—where is the Republican apology?

Folks, the Goldwater era Republican doesn't exist anymore—for one, he was pro-choice and approved of gays in the military—and America wasn't distracted from our real issues, by these wedge issues—and added into the mix by Republicans, today, so the voter will be looking away from what they are REALLY UP TO.

Specifically, the national Republican Party, today, has only ONE program—to pander to the GREED of their wealthiest contributors—PERIOD, That's it—they have NO other program!

In short, folks, turning America over to the current Republican agenda is analogous to handing the keys to our new Cadillac to a fallen-down drunk—who wrecked our car last week—would anyone in touch with reality do this? Don't answer that....

Jim Green, www.Inclusivism.org

CHAPTER SIX

Letter to the editor:

THIS IS A TEST. The following are two political speeches—the question is, were they made by a Republican or a Democrat? Were they made by the same candidate, and if not, what candidate most likely made the respective speeches—and how relevant are the respective speeches to the problems we face today? Don't peek—the answer is at the bottom—

Speech One:

"Folks, we live in an era of great challenge-- our people are a hearty, industrial people—and they can meet that challenge....Industry means employment and that employment means a fair wage for anybody who wants to work—and I mean to see that we get there....".

Speech Two:

"Ladies and Gentlemen, we have met today at a cross-roads— these are not ordinary times—we meet at a cross-roads in history. For far too long the wrong roads have been taken—the wrong roads have led us into war, into poverty, into unemployment and

inflation. May I say to you, we have reached the turning-point—
No longer will 'We the people' suffer for the benefit of the few.

Now I would lie to you if I told you the roads would be easy—
they will not be easy—nothing that is right and good has ever
been easy. 'We the people' know that—and we know the right
roads and the good. Today, I say to you—We are the people, you
and I—and it is time to let the people rule. Thank You"

Speech Two was written for, and given by Charles Palentine, a
fictions candidate for president in the noted movie "Taxi Driver",
a film made in 1976 [36 years ago].

Speech One was made by John M. Staton [a real person and a real
speech]—the Governor of Georgia—the speech was made in
1911 [over 100 years ago—Staton was a Democrat]—

What is that maxim—"The more things change, the more they
stay the same".

Jim Green, Democrat candidate for Congress, 2000

CHAPTER SEVEN

Editor/NYTimes:

Gore Vidal refers to America as the "United States of Amnesia"—
his reference is to how quickly we seem to forget atrocious
government policy--

And the Republican candidates are trying to capitalize on this by
blurring the line regarding our current economic recovery—

Even appealing to those with a short-term memory loss by
hinting that President Obama may have caused our economic
meltdown—even though he had not even been elected president
at that time—

And in their desperation to regain the White House they would
not have anything good to say about President Obama if he had
saved them from drowning—

Serious discussion about real issues—essential to an informed
electorate--gets lost in the minutia—it is little wonder it has been
dubbed the "Silly Season"—

The truth is—"Supply-Side Economics" resulted in atrocious
government policies—that run up massive deficits for our

grandchildren to pay-- drove our economy into a ditch—and all
of the Republican candidates—save for Ron Paul—have told us
they will return to this failed economic model—if elected!

The truth is, our deficit was only $60 billion in 1980—and in
every year since, when Republicans held the White House—they
have added to our deficit, driving it up to a staggering $10 trillion
by the time Bush II left office!

The interest, alone, on this debt is $400 billion annually—almost
2/3rds of our Defense Budget!

Further it is pure bull that Republicans and Democrats share
equally in the disaster caused by Supply-Side—the Democrats
had control of Congress only one year during Reagan's two
terms—the last year—and only the last two years of Bush II, but
by then most of the damage had already been done—and at NO
time did they have sufficient votes to override a presidential
veto—

Further, calling for Republicans to apologize is two-fold. Absent
an apology the Republicans in Congress are arrogant—like they
have pulled off the Brink's robbery and gotten away with it—and
compounded by a press too timid [to be kind] to demand they be
held accountable—and secondly, they have not said anything, up
to now, to affirm that they will not pick up where Bush II left off,

if elected1 In fact, their "no tax increase on the wealthy" is consummate proof of it--

For the Republicans in the House it is "Don't confuse me with facts"—

President Obama was forced to use deficits to clean up the mess caused by the reckless Republicans policies of the past 8 years—it was the only medicine available—according to every credible economist in American, on the right or left1 And McCain would have been forced to take the exact same action—if he wanted to prevent America from going into another Great Depression1

So the "blank check" lie put out by Boehner—suggesting that President Obama is a "tax and spend" liberal—is a contemptible lie1

Further, How on earth can anyone or any political party hold themselves up to the champions in cutting the deficit—WHEN THEIR PARTY CAUSED IT1

Jim Green

CHAPTER EIGHT

President Obama/Fellow Democrats:

For the past 65 years we have had two parallel paths to address unemployment in America—

To assure employment for the troops returning from WW II, President Truman signed into law The Full Employment Act of 1946—

This was expanded upon in 1978 with the Humphrey-Hawkins Full Employment Act, signed into law by President Carter—

And a 21st Century version of this path to full employment in America, is pending the House, HR 870.

Humphrey-Hawkins best defines this path to addressing unemployment in America, and it authorizes our government to create a "reservoir of public employees" anytime our unemployment rises above "3%".

And in spite of the fact that this path to employment has been the law of the land since 1946—and is a Pro-Market solution [more on this shortly]---Washington has lacked the wherewithal to

implement this path to employment on behalf of the American people—[a point not lost on the "occupy" movement].

Rather, Washington has taken the alternate parallel path—by insisting that human labor is a "component" in the free enterprise system—[barely distinguishable from the machine the human operates] to be used and discarded "at will"—and that it is an attack upon "freedom" to challenge this concept, but whose "freedom"?

As a result, however, "conventional wisdom" has insisted that it is the market, alone, that can fix our unemployment crisis—the result has been a disaster—

The market thrives when we have a robust, employed, consuming public—and by taking this parallel path—we not only have a staggering 9% unemployment, but a struggling recovery as well.

Ironically, following WW II, Australia passed a law very similar to our Full Employment Act of 1946—

Difference is—they actually put it into effect—and over the next 30 years—[until the cold winds of conservatism swept in Reagan and Thatcher, etc.] –the government in Australia saw as a solemn responsibility that "anyone willing to work should be provided with a job" [a quote from the "Audacity of Hope"].

The citizens of Australia still refer to this 30 years as their "Golden Age".

Jim Green, Democrat candidate for Congress, 2000
www.Inclusivism.org

CHAPTER NINE

Editor/NY Times:

FDR urged us to put ending unemployment on a war footing—
and it is the failure of the OECD countries to follow the wisdom in
this observation, particularly in Greece, Spain and the U.S.—that
has their economies in trouble today—

A large part of the problem is that we are victims of our own
success—while we have grown more and more efficient in the
marketplace, we have become less efficient with what to do with
the fallout—we celebrate innovation and then are befuddled with
what to do with the 9 persons who are displaced in the workplace
by the innovation—

And in the mid-1970's the colliding mega-forces—automation,
globalization, innovation, technology, etc., reached a critical mass
resulting in ubiquitous unemployment in all of the OECD
countries—

In the U.S. the result was a "malaise"—as we turned to the market
to fix itself—a mind-set that continues to this day—

Over the past 65 years our Congress, and two American presidents [Truman & Carter], have stepped up to the plate and passed laws to end unemployment in America—but inexplicably these laws have never been enforced—

Specifically, the Humphrey-Hawkins Full Employment Act [15 USC § 3101] authorizes the government/president to create a "reservoir of public employees"—at any point in which our unemployment in America rises above "3%" [and we are three times over the percent necessary, at present, to trigger this law]—

But in spite of the fact that it is a Pro-Market solution—[the market thrives when we have a robust, employed, consuming public]—and we can fund without adding a dime to our deficit—an antiquated mind-set has prevented enforcement of these laws—

In short, the world has changed, our solutions haven't, and the result has been a disaster! We are Hell-bent on fixing our unemployment crisis with "private sector jobs"—[a concept antithetical to capitalism]—and the result has been a disaster—

Accordingly, the minute our Debt Ceiling crisis is behind us [the Republicans grow up!]—Congress is urged to pass the Neighbor-To-Neighbor Job Creation Act. A federally mandated, mutual insurance, owned by our employed to provide the funds to hire/train our unemployed, See: www.Inclusivism.org and HR 870 [currently in Committee].

The truism is that fixing unemployment is an indispensable component in fixing an economy—and the proposed, here, is a Pro-Market "win-win" solution—the American people win, and capitalism wins!

Jim Green, Democrat candidate for Congress, 2000

CHAPTER TEN

THE FAIL-SAFE ELECTRONIC VOTING ACT:

So long as the potential for manipulation of electronic voting continues to exist—our elections in America will be in peril! In spite of all the polls showing a strong Obama victory--it was not until 10PM Central on 11-4-08.....that we could breath a sigh of relief....we had been cheated out of the past two elections....with many believing that Bush was never legally elected president of the United States....and we were braced for the worst.......this can, and MUST be fixed before 2010, so that this never happens again, and in the interest of all who support fair and open elections-- regardless of party. Accordingly, it is urged that we adopt the following proposed "FAIL-SAFE ELECTRONIC VOTING ACT":

THE FAIL-SAFE ELECTRONIC VOTING ACT

1) EVERY electronic voting machine (hereafter EVM), must be inexpensive, identical throughout the U.S. in a 1/150 ratio, and *must count and produce a hard-copy of the recorded votes.* In addition, an extra copy of their recorded votes would be produced (not necessarily a hard-copy), marked "Voter's Copy", and containing "NOTICE: Do Not Destroy Until Every Election On Your Ballot Is Certified". [If Wal-Mart handed us a piece of paper with the words "trust us" as a receipt for our purchases—we

would be outraged—and this is our current electronic voting nightmare—but in this case it is our democracy at risk]1

2) *After confirming that their votes are recorded correctly,* the voter would then insert the hard-copy ballot into a software-free (count only) optical scanner (hereafter OS), for a second count. The hard-copy ballot would be retained by election officials in the event a candidate asks for a recount (*not possible under the current system, and which undermines the legality of each such election).* The EVM and the OS must be manufactured by different companies (which is universally true today).

3) Election officials assigned to oversee the EVM, would be prevented by law from overseeing the OS, and vice-versa, and stiff criminal penalties would be imposed for violations.

4) Further, every EVM would be programmed with raw data re the total registration rolls, by party, and norms for their voting history, etc.,----as an "alert" to a possible irregularity, such as an "Under-vote"—or "vote-flipping" etc., and *standards* established to suspend certification where there is an "improbable result", at least temporarily, of a particular election until the discrepancy is cleared up. (This is what computers do best, and it would be very easy to create such a program).

5) At the end of the election day, tallies would be taken from the

EVM and the OS, for each candidate. *If the tallies didn't balance for any given election, or if there is an "alert", that election cannot be certified until the "error" is corrected.* If the candidates agree (the victory is certain), minor discrepancies in the count could be disregarded. While probably rare, the Voter, or a random sample of Voters, would be required by law to return their Copy of the recorded votes to the election office to clear up any "error", or where an "alert" signals the need for same.

6) Further, every state provides for a recount when the total vote falls below a certain percent of difference between the candidates, impossible to conduct with the current EVM—and thus Congress must mandate the following regarding presidential candidates: A RUN-OFF election is mandated and triggered in those states where the percent of total vote is less than .5% of difference between any given candidates; said election to be held on the second Saturday following the election, on PAPER BALLOTS ONLY, and contain ONLY the names of the relevant candidates, for instance: "Barack Obama, Democrat" and "John McCain, Republican"—with oversight in counting by a representative(s) of each party—said procedure providing more than adequate time to meet the Electoral College mandate. NOTE: Had this been the law in 2000, Al Gore would be our president, and the American economy would not be in meltdown!

7) Finally, absent the above safeguards, and until these safeguards are in place--Congress must mandate that PAPER BALLOTS, ONLY, can be used in our presidential elections. This is not a "partisan" issue, it is a "pro-democracy" issue. Most importantly, this will return the responsibility for our elections, and our vote counting, back into the hands of the individual voter, where it belongs, and out of the hands of "corporate control"---*it is after all "our democracy", itself, that is at risk if we don't take these steps---and in that regard, is there any time or cost differential that is too great?*

Jim Green

CHAPTER ELEVEN

FACEBOOK. TO CNN CAFFERTYFILE

Words are cheap! Romney brags that he can "get America
working again"—that he can create 12 million jobs in his first
year---So why is no one in the media asking Romney to
explain—IN VERY SPECIFIC TERMS—exactly how he plans to do
that? In truth, Romney's "method" is identical to Bush's method—
which drove our economy into a ditch—and the American people
need to know this! Jim Green, Democrat candidate for Congress,
2000

CHAPTER TWELVE

WHERE IS THE REPUBLICAN APOLOGY?

Futuristic fables such a "Rollerball" and "The Time Machine"
propose scenarios for where us humans may be headed—

Too bad we don't have scenario with a rewind button, like our
VCR, so we Americans could rewind and correct mistakes we
made in the past—

For instance, let's say Justice Kennedy was ill that Saturday—and
the U.S. Supreme Court didn't shut down the vote counting in
Florida, and Al Gore—as all of the evidence shows to be correct—
was elected president—

President Gore actually listened to the warnings from the CIA,
and Massad [Israel's CIA] in August 2001—and by being on high
alert—9-11 never happened—

No war on Iraq, or Afghanistan or on "terror"—No tens of
thousands of lives lost--No $10 trillion hole for the American
taxpayers to did themselves out----with $400 billion annually
just to pay the interest on this debt, and trillions to mop up the
mess this debt has caused—

And an economy so weakened by this deficit that our ability to dig out of this hole has been severely compromised—

But real tragedy is that absent a Republican apology [at an absolute minimum]—the Republican candidates for president, and in Congress are arrogant—like they pulled off the Brink's robbery and got away with it—

And incredulously that want to blame the Democrats, and America's progress over the past 70 years--for THEIR crimes!

But the most alarming—in the absence of an apology--the Republican agenda has not changed one iota!

It is still cut taxes for their wealthiest contributors, and add the short fall in revenue on to our deficit—they want to continue turning the American Dream, into America's Nightmare!

And absent an apology they intend to pick up right where Bush II left off!

CHAPTER THIRTEEN

To the editor/NY TIMES:

The Romney/Ryan faction are the grandchildren and children, respectively, of those Republicans who hated FDR, have fought Social Security from day one, and have been trying to decimate it for the past 77 years—it raises the question regarding this extremist faction of the Republican Party:

Do they hate old people, Do they hate the disabled—Do they hate everybody?

One thing is certain by the Ryan budget, alone—they want to cut Medicare and give the money to our billionaires!

Further, never has there been a more stark difference between their vision for America's future-

That is, the vision for America, between Republicans and Democrats, could not stand out in more bold relief in this election-----and by putting Ryan on the ticket, Romney put the Republican agenda on a rocket ship straight into the 8th Century!

The Republicans want to roll back almost all of America's social progress of the past 200 years—and with women's rights as a special target—it makes you wonder if questioning their right to vote is just over the horizon?

As the bumper sticker so accurately defines [D] is for drive, and [R] is for reverse—so we have a very clear choice in this election—do we want to go forwards, or backwards?

My choice is [D]emocrat!

Jim Green, Democrat candidate for Congress, 2000 See also: "Why President Obama Lost The 2012 Election" on Amazon/Kindle [written to get our apathetic off their butts and vote for President Obama]

CHAPTER FOURTEEN

A response to the false stereotypes made about Democrats.

I really did like the letter from R L "Wake up Jim Green" —and I
hope this letter will be printed as my response]—because she
touches upon almost all of the stereotypes Republicans like to use
in their talking points, about Democrats—and in not one case do
they get it right—

Here goes. First, it is the Democrats who are concerned with what
is in the best interest of the American people, and America—as
opposed to the agenda of the national Republican Party, who are
SOLELY interested in what is in the best economic interests of
their richest contributors—PERIOD—

They have NO interest in the best economic well being of the
"rank and file" who inexplicably vote Republican for a "national"
office [the House, and above]—the agenda of the national
Republican Party is about pandering to the GREED of their richest
contributors—NOT working to create a better and stronger
America—PERIOD!

Indeed, and as exhibit 1, the Republicans in Congress, today, are
employing a political strategy to trash America—in the hopes that
Obama will be blamed—and they will re-gain the White House—

i.e., to use all extremes available—it is a "political" strategy that presumes the American people are really dumb—and it may backfire--

There is nuance in the specifics of my response—to quote: "Democrats have piddled away our tax dollars long enough pandering to political cronies and subsidizing 'free' give away programs to procure votes....".

There are several layers in this opinion—I'll take them one at a time, but not in sequence.

First we need to keep in mind that "projection" is a term used in Psychology—it is projecting, or ascribing OUR motives on to others—blaming them for OUR motives.

It was not the Democrats, but rather the Tea Party Republicans in Congress who played "politics" by taking America to the brink of bankruptcy—and losing our AAA credit rating in the world community!

These Republicans were running out the back door—TO AVOID PAYING BILLS THEY HAD CREATED! Raising the debt ceiling is to pay for bills we have already incurred—

It was the Republicans, alone, who doubled our deficit from $5 trillion to $10 trillion [the bills, above, they were trying to avoid paying]--during Bush II—they controlled all three branches of our government from 2001 to 2007—

And even when the American people regained their senses, and gave a majority of the House back to the Democrats, it was already too late—and Democrats also could not over-ride a presidential veto to stop this reckless and dangerous spending by the Republicans!

The [Democrats] "piddled away our tax dollars long enough" is interesting—

A popular pundit had as a stock question of Republican guests on his program, "Tell me what programs you would cut"? —and invariably they would get the same fumbleitis as Perry during the Republican debates—

For instance, should we do away with the Defense Department? By far, we spend more on our Defense/Intelligence community— than any other part of our federal budget—approaching $2 trillion annually--

Social Security Insurance has always been a "red herring"—which the Republicans derisively call an "entitlement" [is this one of the "give away" programs you are referring to Ms. L?]—

Social Security is an INSURNACE—it brings in more than it pays out—it does not add a dime to our deficit—and is very similar to our auto insurance—do you refer to your auto insurance as an "entitlement"?

Finally, Ms. L said that Democrats are motivated in creating programs, such as the GI Bill, Social Security Insurance, etc., to "procure votes"—WRONG—this is solely the province of the national Republican Party—

It is they who want you to distract the voters by having them talk about gay marriage, or gays in the military, etc., so they can tear down the EPA, and the Republicans have introduced 160 bills since January to undermine the protection of our environment—and for one reason: GREED!

What the "rank and file" who vote Republican don't seem to understand about our "Greed-Driven"—those have bought and paid for the Republicans in Congress—want your vote, alright—but meet them on the street and they would treat you like dirt on their shoes—and under their breath they call you jerks, and they think you are stupid—and given the facts---oh well, you figure it out....

Greed is like pornography, Ms. L—it has no socially redeeming value—

Jim Green

CHAPTER FIFTEEN

Editor/NYTimes:

Why have we gone nuts over paying taxes?

I never cease to be amazed how supportive and emotion-neutral we are in pooling our money for the benefit of all—when it comes to paying our auto insurance, or homeowner's insurance—

But go apoplectic and are emotion-charged when it comes to pooling our money for the benefit of all—when it comes to paying "taxes"—[Is it possible that paying taxes been soured by propaganda—by those who don't want to pay any—like the 1%]?

Also, tt seems to have something to do with "power"—[The rank and file Republicans appear to have contempt for Democrats, solely, because they win—like hating the opposing team if their team loses....rather than a concern for the betterment of America]...

We don't see people saying I am going to cancel my car insurance because claims are being paid to persons who are "black, or brown, or different, or just other humans"—but Republicans suddenly become xenophobic when it comes to paying taxes--

Also, some are OK so long as the taxes are going for Defense and prisons—but outraged when it goes out being our "brother's keeper"--

And we can't exclude propaganda-driven "greed" from the mix—

In short, we are all over the map when it comes to paying taxes—but are silent when it comes to paying our auto insurance—indeed, compulsory auto insurance is law [demanded by the public] in almost every country in the world, including the U.S.--

Jim Green, Democrat candidate for Congress, 2000

CHAPTER SIXTEEN

Editor/NYTimes,

The Republican invented term "American Exceptionalism"—is for losers....

I don't know about the rest of you but I find the new term used in right-wing propaganda—"American Exceptionalism"—and used quite frequently during the Republican debates—to be a particularly disturbing term—

For one, I have never met anyone yet who truly was "exceptional" –who found it necessary call themselves that—and conversely, it is spot-on correct in identifying persons who are suffering from low self-esteem—and prop themselves up by boasting—

Further, other countries looking at America, and coming to that conclusion—or not reaching this conclusion—are quite capable of reaching that conclusion on their own—without our finding it necessary to remind them—

And it has a particularly negative tone by suggesting to other countries—to borrow from a psychological term in "Games People Play"—"Mine's bigger than yours"—

Finally, the term is particularly disturbing because it suggests that as a world power—we are history—or at best, on our way out—and that calling ourselves "exceptional" is a last ditch, desperate grasp to remind other countries that we are the big cheese----

And the sooner this term is in the trash bin of history, the better— IMHO

Jim Green, Democrat candidate for Congress, 2000 [See also: My Letters To President Obama, on Amazon/Kindle]

CHAPTER SEVENTEEN

Editor/NYTimes.

I don't know about the rest of you but I am fed-up with all of the negative blather by the Republican candidates for president—against President Obama—

President Obama was handed a nightmare when he came into office—an economy in free-fall, and in the worst crash since the Great Depression.

What our expert economists [on the right and left] learned from the Great Depression is that the only prescription available is for our government to infuse cash, and plenty of it, into the economy to unfreeze an economy that had seized up—

It is the reason why the Bush administration infused almost a trillion dollars in TARP funds into our economy in 2008—and a like amount in "stimulus" money was appropriated by the Obama administration in early 2009—

And it is the exact same strategy that was used by the Reagan administration in 1987 when the stock market crashed on "Black Monday" resulting an almost 25% loss in one day—

During the Great Depression the FED concluded that to stop the Crash in 1929, that we should pull cash out of the economy—it was a terrible blunder—and accelerated our economic free-fall—turning what might have been a short-term recession, into the Great Depression it took us years to dig out of—

It is the reason every credible economist today urged the "stimulus" moneys President Obama used to prevent another Great Depression—

Politics being what they are, however, Republican strategists decided to appeal to our ignorant an uninformed by painting the "stimulus" used by President Obama—as wild spending by a "tax and spend" liberal—and this distorted lie persists by the Republican candidates for president to this day!

Also, it is unseemly and hypocritical for these candidates, as well as all of the Republicans in Congress, to now claim to be the champions of "deficit reduction"—WHEN IT IS REPUBLICAN POLICIES that handed President Obama a $10 trillion deficit when he came into office!

And to top it off the only solution offered by Republicans is to return to the same policies—THAT CAUSED OUR ECONOMIC MELTDOWN IN 2008—and the Republican One and Only job creations solution is based on the "Big Lie"!

It would be impossible to have 14 million Americans still unemployed if cutting taxes for the wealthy created jobs—BECAUSE THE BUSH TAX CUTS WERE EXTENDED!

So the next time Romney/Ryan demonize President Obama—remind them that they are Lying Hypocrites—and are stuffed between ears with rice pudding!

Jim Green, Democrat candidate for Congress, 2000
www.Inclusivism.org

CHAPTER EIGHTEEN

Editor/NY Times.

Where did these people come from, and why are they voting
Republican?

The Republican Party has been mining our radical religious right,
our racists, and our ignorant [per Ron Reagan], since the civil
rights act of 1964—and they have doubled down since we now
have a "black" president—

But when we superimpose an "economic representation" map
over who the Republican Party represents—and the above
faction—the overlap is zilch! Maybe one or two out of millions
will show up in both maps!

Were a "representative" government folks. We hire people [our
politicians] who "have our back"—to use a popular phrase—
persons who are "in our corner"—and the agenda of the national
Republican Party is to pander to the GREED of their wealthiest
contributors-- PERIOD!

In short, they don't "represent" this faction—thus leaving the
question—why would anyone in this faction who is in their right
mind vote for a political party that doesn't "represent" them? [and

please don't add "because they are not in their right mind"—the problem is far too serious for levity]….

But this is where it really gets interesting—with the Republicans Party's high dive into the abyss—and the two feeding off of each other—i.e., the Republican Party has become a magnet for candidates who want women barefoot, pregnant and in the kitchen—and with Paul Ryan and Congressman Akin, as Exhibit One!

Indeed, in adding Ryan to the ticket, Romney has strapped his agenda in this election to a rocket ship—straight into the 8th Century! And his energy plan for "drill baby drill" would send our melting ice cap into overdrive!

The bottom line is: Never has there been a more stark difference in the direction the respective parties want to take America—It's [D] for drive, and [R] for reverse—i.e., the Democrats want to move FORWARD into the 21st Century, while Romney wants to take us BACK to the Dark Ages!

Jim Green, Democrat candidate for Congress, 2000 [See also: "My Letters To President Obama" and "Why President Obama Lost The 2012 Election: A Wake-Up Call"—on Amazon/Kindle

CHAPTER NINETEEN

Editor/NYTimes.

Folks---We need to pull back the curtain and look at what is really behind the Republican agenda in this election.

First, we have tiny, tiny, tiny handful of Americans who are willing to chip in over a billion dollars to get Romney/Ryan elected—

And we need to drill down on who these folks are, and ask what do they want? For one, these are business people—they are not going to gamble that kind of cash unless they plan on getting a payoff for their gamble—

And their payoff, folks, is to have their taxes cut even further—so they can turn their billion dollars, into two billion—and not just via the tax cuts but also by hiding their cash in tax sheltered accounts in the Cayman Islands, etc., rather than investing in America, ad nauseam!

In short, folks—if this tiny, tiny, tiny handful [the 1%] is chipping in over a billion dollars to get Romney/Ryan elected--the last candidates us 99% should be voting for—is Romney/Ryan!

Jim Green, Democrat candidate for Congress, 2000

CHAPTER TWENTY

Editor/NYTimes:

Every informed voter needs to ask in this election:

Why on earth did America allow itself to be painted into the extreme, and radical position that if you are not an Adam Smith capitalist—you're a communist?

It is a position as hysterical as McCarthyism—and equally as dangerous—

There is little dispute, anywhere, that America turned down this dark alley when the U.S. Supreme Court gave corporations a blank check to buy our elections!

And "Super Pacs" started cropping up all over the place, and the Norquist Pledge—threatening persons running for Congress— "raise taxes, and we will spend millions to defeat you"—

AND NO accountability to disclose the source of their funds!

We got our first taste of this corrupt buying of our elections in 2010—when the House was bought and paid for with this "blood money" ["money gotten ruthlessly at the expense of others' suffering"]—and in this case the victims are the American people↑

For instance, this new crop of radicals in the House have introduced 160 bills [and counting] since January 2011—to destroy our environmental protection laws—so that corporations can drill the Rocky Mountains down to an ant hill↑↑

And they have made crystal clear that they intend to use the American people as a battering ram—under the devious political agenda to undermine President Obama—

It as contemptible, as well as hypocritical, by claiming to now be the champion of deficit reduction—when it Republican policy THAT CAUSED THE DEFICIT↑

Jim Green, Democrat candidate for Congress, 2000

CHAPTER TWENTY-ONE

Editor/NYTimes:

Mitch McConnell said after the debt ceiling talks at the White House on July 10, 2011—that it is "baffling that the president and his party continue to insist on massive tax hikes in the middle of a jobs crisis."

Is there anyone with half a brain in America who cannot see that this statement is a phony as three-dollar bill?

First, the "massive" he is talking about is Exxon giving up the $5 billion in subsidies they got from us, the American people—while sticking it to us at the pump—and recording the highest profits in American history—for starters!

But here is the real con job in that statement—the "Big Lie" being perpetrated on the American people by the Republicans in Congress is that tax cuts for the wealthy will magically translate into jobs!

Well hey, Senator McConnell the Bush tax cuts were extended so why do we have 14 million Americans still unemployed—where are all those jobs that you promised us if we continued the Bush tax cuts last December?

And why were 10 times more private sector jobs created when Clinton was president—and the tax rates on the most wealthy was raised from 35% to 39%--than at any time during the entire Bush II presidency?

McConnell said that his single objective from the day President Obama was elected—was to prevent his re-election in the 2012 election [consummate proof that McConnell had no interest in working on behalf of the American people]—but since President Obama had no record which would justify this judgment by McConnell—is there any explanation other than McConnell is a racist pig—and that he was speaking to his like kind.....?

So why don't we tell the truth in America? And where is our media in calling McConnell out on this racist statement?

Jim Green, Democrat candidate for Congress, 2000

CHAPTER TWENTY-TWO

Editor/NY Times:

Doesn't it strike anyone as odd that Paul Ryan rails, daily, over deficits under President Obama—indeed, holding himself out, now, as a champion of deficit reduction—WHEN he voted to drive up our deficit by over $7 trillion, while in Congress, under Bush II!

Actually, "odd" may be too kind—maybe "disingenuous" [which is the polite way to say someone is a lying SOB]—"Aw shucks" , Ryan is a lying hypocrite—it is the only honest description that fits!

And to add insult to injury, Ryan now wants to decimate [i.e., destroy] Medicare—[read Ryan's Budget]--so he can give the money saved to the Republican's wealthiest contributors—their payoff for getting him elected! What a guy!

We won't even go to his Draconian approach regarding "women's rights", [including being anti-choice]—and evident by his co-sponsoring legislation with Akin, Ad Nauseam!

And he is doing all of this while claiming to be a "Christian" [actually Catholic]—seems he has forgotten that if one is not following the teachings of Christ, one is NOT a Christian! Which the "Nuns On A Bus" have been quick to remind him!

And if the reader does not know that the sole agenda of the National Republican Party, the same as Ryan, is to make the rich, richer—and them poorer—they are not paying attention!

But getting back to the deficit, please consider this metaphor. If one of our children spills a glass of milk—we wipe it up with some paper towels—but if they spill a whole gallon—we grab a mop and a bucket and everything else at hand to clean up the mess—

And, President Obama was handed a mega-spill to clean up—from day one—as a direct result of the mess caused by Ryan, and the rest of the Republicans over the past 8 years!

In short, it cost us—the American taxpayers $5 trillion just to clean up the $10 trillion mess left by the Republicans, i.e., it was this "mop and bucket" President Obama had to use to prevent another Great Depression!

Finally, you would think Romney and company would, first, profusely apologize to the American people for the mess they left—and then promise never to pull this gimmick on the American people again—

But they have the gall to tell us they are going to double-down—
i.e., pick up right where Bush II left off!

 Do they think we are stupid? Don't answer that....

Jim Green, Democrat candidate for Congress, 2000 [See also. "My
Letters To President Obama", and "Why President Obama Lost The
2012 Election. A wake-up call", on Amazon/Kindle

CHAPTER TWENTY-THREE

Editor/NYTimes,

What we have learned from the Republican primaries—is that a tiny, tiny handful of Americans have crowded the Republican Party into a such a reactionary and radical corner that it has become like a Black Hole in space—so impacted by extremism that light can barely escape—

And we know this by what they are talking about as "issues"—and by how few Americans are showing up to vote—

For instance, in Maine ALL of the Republican candidates received only one-half of one percent of those eligible to vote—99.5 % were absentee—as one pundit observed, the "R" in Republican has come to mean "Racists and Radicals", i.e., they are the only ones who are showing up to vote—

Regarding issues—women are not to use contraceptives—and if they get pregnant [even if via a rape] they cannot terminate the pregnancy—in short they want to put "Rosie the Riveter" back in the kitchen—barefoot and pregnant—can ending her right to vote be far behind?

Also, another pundit observed--98% of women use contraceptives, and the other 2% are lying—even disregarding that it is patently irresponsible given our teen pregnancy, and married or unmarried, to venture into parenthood in the reckless method this Republican policy advocates!

Also, the lack of civility in our current political discourse has become so coarsened as to be alarming.

To make the distinction, war hero and former Senator Bob Dole said it best when he said President Clinton is "My opponent, not my enemy"—but much of the rhetoric today is an appeal to persons who want to de-humanize President Obama.

In short, being critical of bad policy, as above, is essential to our getting good government—de-humanizing a person, or group, is the tactic used to carry out the Holocaust—

The truth is, President Obama was handed a nightmare, and he deserves a solid "A" for what he got right—i.e., the vitriolic rhetoric is baseless, devoid of logic or the facts—and has cheapened even "political" prattle--

And it is unthinkable that we would hand America back to the spineless Republicans—who have placed "politics" [appealing to these nuts cases]—over what is in the best interests of America!

In short, we have a tiny handful of racists and radicals in the Republican Party drowning out any semblance of sanity and civility in our political discourse, today—and a 24-7 news cycle handing them the mic--so they can sell soap—i.e., will "Greed and Ignorance" finally do us in?

Jim Green, Democrat candidate for Congress, 2000
www.Inclusivism.org

CHAPTER TWENTY-FOUR

Editor/NYTimes:

A number of our new congresspersons are threatening to dismantle the healthcare reforms by the Democrats [which actually didn't go far enough]—but we need to ask, why on earth would they even consider doing this?

The only persons complaining about the reforms made by Democrats to our healthcare system—are persons who do not understand the healthcare system we have now [and this can also be said about many of the reforms over the past 2 years]—

For instance, America is the only country in the world that permits their health insurance companies to make a "profit" off of people getting healthcare—

After all, our health insurance companies don't even so much as put a Band-Aid on a patient—they are simply a pass-through agent—we pool our money to brace against the high costs of healthcare, if we need it [as with all other insurance] and they pay out our claims--[and as a footnote, a metaphor we should adopt in paying taxes—where we pool our money for our individual protection, and for the common good]--

As it has turned out our health insurance companies have turned this "pass through" thing they do—not just into a way to make a little money in the process—but rather into a Texas-sized bonanza---a gold mine at the expense of our health--this is not a big business—it is a big, big, big business—with obscene salaries for their CEO's, etc—

For instance, our health insurance companies have six lobbyists for each of the 435 Members of Congress, and 100 members of the Senate—all with six figure salaries--as I write—and all are there for only one reason—to protect the pot of gold the health insurance companies are making off of the American people!

But the real wake-up call—for those who do not understand the reforms made by the Democrats—every dime of those salaries to lobbyists came from money they sent in in premiums—money intended for the healthcare of Americans, not to enrich the health insurance companies!

This also explains why we are 37th in the world in the quality of healthcare in America, according to the World Health Organization—and we have a mortality rate along side some Third World countries!

In summing up—and for clarity---sell a car, make a buck—
absolutely, that is the America way—but making a "profit" off of
people's health should be a criminal offense—

Jim Green, Democrat candidate for Congress, 2000
www.Inclusivism.org

CHAPTER TWENTY-FIVE

I saved the best for last [I couldn't resist including this].... This chapter is dedicated to our Teavangelicals, and assorted nuts courted by the Republican Party—and which are, at best, strange bedfellows—because it is impossible to be Christian—and vote for anything the Republicans stand for.

A MESSAGE FROM GOD

MANY CENTURIES AGO, a man of the cloth, we don't know his name, and in a flash of insight (perhaps induced by peyote) told his flock that "sex is a sin". And lo and behold he learned that by taking a very natural and healthy part of our life and turning it into something that was "dirty and nasty", that he could imprison his flock, and fill his coffers, and hallelujah it was a great day for the Lord!

Quickly, his miracle spread to other churches in his village, and then to the next village, and then the next county and then state and then it spread to all the churches in the ancient world, and all of their flocks cowed in fear and shame and became imprisoned, and their coffers over-floweth. Hallelujah, it was a great day for the Lord!

And to keep the myth alive they started inventing stories, half-baked stories, that made no sense to anyone who is rational, such as "Mary was a virgin"—well, she just had to be a virgin because she would never partake in anything that was dirty and nasty, like sex (if you're doing it right), and this was necessary to make "sex is a sin" make sense...so they invented a Mary that was "sinless"--you get the picture. And it is apparent that God had to make sex very pleasurable just to overcome all the bullshit. And their coffers over-floweth. Hallelujah, it was a great day for the Lord!

No one seemed to be bothered that when we play tricks on the human mind by taking something that is very natural and healthy, such as sex, and make it dirty and nasty that all kinds of bad things happen to the human mind.

Such as most pedophiles, and most serial killers, and voting Republican, and unwarranted suicides, and most mental illness, and unwanted pregnancies. (Teens not wanting to have sex is the perversion, not the other way around, and by replacing sex education and condoms, with unrealistic "abstinence", and by using blather about "low self-esteem" to shame them into not "sinning"--We have a teen pregnancy in the U.S. twice that of England and Canada!).

But none of this mattered, because their coffers over-floweth, and Hallelujah, it is a great day for the Lord!

There is a cure———————Tell these right-wing loonies to shove it....

GOD

ANTHOLOGY II

MY LETTERS TO PRESIDENT OBAMA. Confessions of a
Compulsive Letter Writer

PROLOGUE

Best guess is that I have written in excess of 500 letters, and
counting, to President Obama since he was sworn in on January
20, 2009—on some occasions I have written two letters in one
day—this is a sampling of those letters.

Compulsive letter writers, incidentally, do not go looking for a
computer/word-processor—they look up and one magically
appears before them—and more often than not they have no idea
how they got there [only a slight exaggeration]—

While my letters to President Obama contain suggestions as well
as constructive criticism—it needs to be said at the beginning that
never in a million years would I vote to put a Republican back in
the White House!

The agenda of the national Republican Party has not changed one
iota since 1980—and has, singularly, brought on all of the
symptoms characteristic during the Fall of The Roman Empire—

i.e., their corrupt and unworkable policies have almost destroyed America!

The best explanation I can find for why anyone would vote for a Republican for president [apparently Romney] was offered by Gore Vidal who observed that we are the "United States of Amnesia"—

We have a segment of Americans who are racists and would never vote for President Obama because he is black—but another component in this "anti-Obama" faction are persons with a severe memory loss [all else being equal] and have forgotten the destruction done to America—by Bush's appointment to the presidency!

If America does fail it will have two parents: GREED and IGNORANCE—Greed on the part of the 1%, and Ignorance on the part of those in the 99%--who are ignorant of the Republican agenda to replace our Democracy, with a Plutocracy—[i.e., to relegate American to the 8th Century]-

And with the five unscrupulous Republican ideologues on our Supreme Court--who sold our democracy, and America, down the river by handing a blank check to the 1% in "Citizens United"—The 1% can now, theoretically, buy our elections and put a dictator, or a common thief, in the White House—

This Decision has gutted our current election laws in America, and the outcome of this horrid Decision is a glaring unknown—its mere existence may well signal that American is finished!

Regarding constructive criticism of the Obama Administration—the criticism has focused on essential changes in two major areas [one barely on the Radar, the other in the headlines daily].

Specifically, the establishment of "Fail-Safe" electronic voting in every jurisdiction in America; and Jobs.

Admittedly, the Administration was forced to spend every waking moment focused on rescuing America from the corrupt and disastrous Republican policies which almost drove our economy into another Great Depression--

But we had a very narrow window when the Democrats controlled the Senate, House and White House and had the opportunity to fix the above—but blew it--and the failure to do so cost the Democrats the 2010 election—and may well cost President Obama re-election to the White House in 2012—

The letters to follow will articulate both the problem, and the proposed solution—[one is a Letter to the editor]—the objective is to communicate re topical issues....

But to touch briefly on the need for "fail-safe" electronic voting machines [hereafter EVM]—what we currently have is a nightmare—With the EVM manufacturers claiming proprietary ownership of the software to count our votes—with known computer manipulation such as "vote-flipping" and "under-votes", and with one manufacturer making a $200, 000 contribution to Bush in 2004, and "guaranteeing" Bush Ohio in 2004! And to top it off--no paper trail for a legitimate recount, or to verify how we voted!

To use a metaphor:

Visualize that Wal-Mart handed us a piece of paper with the words "trust us" as a receipt for our purchases—and you will have a consummate understanding of our current electronic voting, in America—In short, did Kerry really lose in 2004—are you really sure? And did the Republicans really give the Democrats a "shellacking" in 2010?

If Wal-Mart did this, incidentally, we would be outraged—but unfortunately far too many Americans are ignorant [or too trusting] of the dangers indigenous to this EVM nightmare—and yet, there is far more at stake than a complaint with Wal-Mart--it is our democracy that is on the chopping block in this case!

Incidentally, the caption on my letters to President Obama almost always read. President Obama/Fellow Democrats, and concluded with Jim Green, Democrat candidate for Congress, 2000—which I hoped would give it at least a little more chance of being read—by anyone—[also, the quoted unemployment rate was current at the time—letters are not in sequence].

Also, initially, I addressed to F. Michael Kelleher—Special assistant to President Obama who sorted out letters for President Obama to read—but letters, there, are limited to 2500 words—and I couldn't get all I wanted to say in, and also include the address to Mr. Kelleher—so had to abbreviate my salutation, as above. [Reader. Please look for the nuggets, if you sense redundancy]....Finally, I have no idea if any of my letters were ever read by President Obama.

CHAPTER ONE: Jobs

President Obama/Fellow Democrats:

For the past 65 years we have had two parallel paths to address unemployment in America—

To assure employment for the troops returning from WW II, President Truman signed into law The Full Employment Act of 1946—

This was expanded upon in 1978 with the Humphrey-Hawkins Full Employment Act, signed into law by President Carter—

And a 21st Century version of this path to full employment in America, is pending the House, HR 870.

Humphrey-Hawkins best defines this path to addressing unemployment in America, and it "authorizes" our government to create a "reservoir of public employees" anytime our unemployment rises above "3%".

And in spite of the fact that this path to employment has been the law of the land since 1946—and is a Pro-Market solution [more on this shortly]---Washington has lacked the wherewithal to

implement this path to employment on behalf of the American people—[a point not lost on the "occupy" movement].

Rather, Washington has taken the alternate parallel path—by insisting that human labor is a "component" in the free enterprise system—[barely distinguishable from the machine the human operates] to be used and discarded "at will"—and the Republican propaganda is that it is an attack upon "freedom" to challenge this concept, but whose "freedom"?

As a result, however, "conventional wisdom" has insisted that it is the market, alone, that can fix our unemployment crisis—the result has been a disaster—

The market thrives when we have a robust, employed, consuming public—and by taking this parallel path—we not only have a staggering 8.1% unemployment, but a struggling recovery as well.

Ironically, following WW II, Australia passed a law very similar to our Full Employment Act of 1946—

Difference is—they actually put it into effect—and over the next 30 years—[until the cold winds of conservatism swept in Reagan and Thatcher, etc.] –the government in Australia saw as a solemn responsibility that "anyone willing to work should be provided with a job" [a quote from the "Audacity of Hope"].

The citizens of Australia still refer to this 30 years as their "Golden Age".

Jim Green, Democrat candidate for Congress, 2000
www.Inclusivism.org

Editor, NY TIMES

The only way any person could "disapprove" of the way President Obama is handling the job—are persons who have not informed themselves with the facts—or are suffering from severe amnesia—or both—

Republican policies had handed President Obama an economy in shambles when he took office in 2009—and we had lost 2.6 million jobs in 2008, alone, the highest job loss in six decades!

We can't siphon America's wealth out of the hands of the consuming middle, the 99%--and transfer it into the hands of the Republican's wealthiest contributors, the 1% [via obscene tax cuts]—without sending our economy into meltdown.

This is based on common sense—The consuming middle stops buying the products made by our manufacturers, when they don't have enough money—and in the domino effect our manufacturers lay off their employees when they don't have consumers for their products—and on and on until our economy is in shamble.

And those who inform themselves know that Reaganomics [what Bush I called "VooDoo economics"] has a shelf-life of about seven years before the economy collapses—as it did in 1987, and again in 2008—

And the taxpayers have to rush in with tons of cash, as Bush did with TARP in 2008, and an equal amount by President Obama--to prevent another Great Depression.

Also, with each new cycle of this economic scheme—the bail out has grown larger and larger—

For instance, in 1987—when the stock market lost one-fourth of its value on Black Monday, October 19, 1987—the bailout was in the hundreds of billions—in 2008, the bailout has been in the trillions of dollars, and counting--to mop up the mess caused by this failed economic agenda!

In short, President Obama did not spend the tons of cash [and as Bush did with TARP]—because he is a wild "tax and spend" liberal—and as our racists and Republican ideologues would have our uninformed believe—

Both Obama and Bush went to the only doctor in town for a prescription [cash and plenty of it] to rescue America from another Great Depression!

Further, when any of the Republicans in Washington rail against our deficit, who voted to cause it—as Paul Ryan did under Bush II—is a hypocrite!

Romney has made it clear, in no uncertain terms, that he intends to pickup where Bush II left off—i.e., to pander to the GREED of the Republican's richest contributors at the expense of the 99% rest of us—it is the Republican One and Only program—

Jim Green, Democrat candidate for Congress, 2000 [see THE HARVARD BOYS CLUB, on Amazon]

President Obama/Fellow Democrats:

Who thought up the idea that the "Market" could solve our unemployment crisis?

The greatest enemy to our economic recovery is the archaic mind-set that it is ONLY the "Market" that can create jobs—

It has been a stumbling block to job creation—

It has been a stumbling block to market recovery—

It may also be a stumbling block to President Obama's re-election—

Going forward—the market will not provide enough jobs, which bears repeating—

Going forward—the market will not provide enough jobs—

Which raises the question: Does the government [under law "We The People"] have a responsibility to step up on behalf of the American people when the market does not provide enough jobs?

And according to the vast majority of "We The People" —"anybody willing to work should be able to find a job" [and the message loud and clear by the "occupy" movement]—

In short, the answer to that question is a resounding, YES

What apparently isn't clear going forward is that an expanding and contracting public workforce is an INDISPENSABLE component to a modern market economy—

This is a Pro-Market "win-win" solution—the American people win, and capitalism wins—

Jim Green, Democrat candidate for Congress, 2000
www.Inclusivism.org YouTube, JGREEN56789

President Obama/Fellow Democrats:

I am a fan. I am 110% in favor of Democrats succeeding—and in a post mortem:

Had we fixed unemployment, everything we did over the past two years would have been seen only in a most positive light [and the Tea Party would have been holding their rallies in a phone booth]—but when we failed to fix—we were seen as not being able to do anything right!

To fix our unemployment crisis in America, we must totally remove the problem from our market economy model—and look upon it, as we rightfully should—as a "social" problem, in search of a social solution—

That is, in looking for a solution, no differently than our methodology for seeking better ways to educate our youth, or fight disease—a social problem in search of a solution—and the sooner we alter direction, the better—

For instance, our current solutions [HR 2847, etc., --warmed over Reaganomics]—look upon humans as a "commodity", rather than an "asset" –and the result of going down this path has been a disaster, and has resulted in our unemployment crisis getting even worse!

This erroneous path also cost the Democrats the House, and resulted in a greatly weakened Senate, in the mid-terms!

A very clear mandate from the public in 2008 was FIX UNEMPLOYMENT—and when the Democrats failed to do this [mostly as a result of bad advice]—the public turned their back on the Democrats, and saw us as weak or incompetent, or both!

And all the while we had the solution at our fingertips in a win/win solution [both the public and capitalism wins]—in the pro-market Humphrey-Hawkins Full Employment Act which authorizes the government/president to create a "reservoir of public employment" anytime our unemployment in America exceeds "3%"—

And we are three times over the percent necessary to trigger this Federal Law—[at 9.8% unemployment]—but can fix overnight without adding a dime to our deficit—www.Inclusivism.org— had we taken the right path]!

And all of our errors could have been avoided from day one had we looked upon unemployment as a "social" problem—in search

of a social solution---in short, we Democrats had our chance—
and we muffed it—

Jim Green, Democrat candidate for Congress, 2000

President Obama/Fellow Democrats:

In his new book "The Grand Design", Stephen Hawking observed,"
To understand the universe at its deepest level, we need to know
not only how the universe behaves, but why."

And the same is true to answer why did we take the wrong path
to address our unemployment crisis in America—[and paid
dearly at the polls --it is impossible to have 9-17%
unemployment and even remotely suggest that we are on the
right path]!

And the question posed here is: Why did our "brightest and
best"—AKA "conventional wisdom" unwittingly take the Obama
administration down the wrong path [HR 2847—failed
Reaganomics]—all [except Republicans] wanted Obama to
succeed in fixing unemployment—

This is one man's opinion re the why our "brightest and best" got
it so wrong.

First and foremost, they have a mental blinder to seeing any
avenue to fix unemployment—except "via the market"—[i.e.,
classical economics—based on the "dollar' rather than on
"humans"]—and even though the path we should be on is

virtually right under their nose-- because of blinders—it is impossible for them to see it--

That is, they are looking for a solution through a false prism—the false prism is that jobs can only be created, as noted, via the "market"—when, in fact, the "market" is the worst place for us to look to solve our unemployment crisis—

For instance, fixing unemployment is antithetical to the objectives of capitalism—unemployment is a "social" problem—and the objectives of capitalism is to make a "profit" –the market only hires persons as a means to increase profits—not to address social problems--

Indeed, every waking moment in capitalism is spent pondering ways to eliminate as many of us humans, as possible, from the workplace—to increase "profits"--

Another illustration of our "brightest and best" being blind-sided—Dr. Robert B. Reich is a progressive—and yet in his book "The Work of Nations"—he does not make even one reference to the Humphrey-Hawkins Full Employment Act—which authorizes the government to create a "reservoir of public employment" anytime our unemployment exceeds "3%"— see also: www.Inclusivism.org

That is, he failed to understand that this IS the answer—this is the path we should be on to fix an unemployment crisis because it is an indispensable component to a modern market economy...it is a pro-market solution--that is, it is a "win-win" solution--the people win, and capitalism wins....

Jim Green, Democrat candidate for Congress, 2000

Reagan was a horrible prez—so why the LIES?

President Obama/Fellow Democrats,

What are we to make of a president who wanted to do the right thing—and probably thought [most of the time] he was doing the right thing—but, in fact, was a horrible president—and, in fact, did substantial harm to America—

The mystery president--and evident by the HBO movie by the same name "Reagan"—who was, without question, the worst president in American history--until Bush II came along and bumped him out of last place—

Problem is—Conservatives/Republicans are currently trying to re-write history—to give us—THE AMERICAN PEOPLE—a pure BS image of Reagan—one where he is elevated to sainthood—it is the "Big Lie"—

Indeed, on this very day [3-2-2011] House Majority Leader Eric Cantor was still trying to pull the wool over the eyes of the American people with the same BS line used re Reaganomics,

Eliminate all of the social progress since FDR, and cut, even further, taxes on the top 2% [the only people Cantor—or any of

the other Republicans in Congress Represent—they certainly do
not represent the best interests of the 98% rest of us Americans]—

But if we do this jobs will flow like wine—

What a CROCK---in short, Cantor wants to slam on the brakes
during a sluggish recovery—which, with a virtual certainty, will
destroy our recovery and destroy jobs in America! Reaganomics
has a shelf-life of about 7 years before the evaporation of wealth
from the consuming middle, and its false premise starts caving in
on itself. Proof-1987/2008

So when are the Democrats going to stand up and have the guts
to say—NO MORE—no more "me too"--no more Reagan lies—no
more harming America—and stand up on behalf of the American
people?

We can end our unemployment crisis in the next 6 months—[
See: www.Inclusivism.org] --but we have to stand up—we have
to show some backbone—show some spine—When are we
Democrats going to stand up and tell the American people the
truth—that Reaganomics is DooDoo BRAINS!

Jim Green, Democrat candidate for Congress, 2000

WHERE IS OUR "UN-AMERICAN" INVESTIGATION INTO THE
REPUBLICAN AGENDA? WHERE IS THE REPUBLICAN APOLOGY?

President Obama/Fellow Democrats.

We need to restore the "Un-American Activities Committee" and
put the Republicans in the Senate and House, et al -- on trial for
selling out the American people, and America--by pandering to
the GREED of their richest contributors—their One and Only
program!

For instance, the Republican "job creation" solution, today, is the
same old cruel joke they have been perpetrating on the American
people since the first Bush tax cuts in 2001—

The joke goes like this. Pour obscene tons of cash [the taxpayers
money] on our richest contributors—and they will use the money
to give everyone a job—supposedly in the corporation—

Well, if this worked—why do we have 14 million Americans still
unemployed? [The Bush tax cuts were extended]!

What really happened is that their richest contributors used the
obscene windfall of cash to buy a bigger yacht, or take extra trips

to Europe—rather than create jobs—as their wealth doubled at the expense of the 98% of the rest of us Americans!

And it makes you wonder how the Republicans in the Senate and House can espouse this joke with a straight face! Fool me once---
-

Further, we learned from this that siphoning America's wealth from our consuming middle has a shelf-life of about 7 years before our economy goes into a nosedive—[1987 & 2008]—and in 2008 brought us dangerously close to another Great Depression!

And compounded by the fact that the Republicans ran up massive deficits on Americans, when they have held the White House since 1980—to make up for the shortfall in revenue—creating a dual crisis. Massive debt as well as high unemployment—and has put America in extreme economic peril!

In short, the current Republican agenda poses far more of threat to Americans, and America—than terrorists!

If this isn't the quintessential definition of "un-American", what is? And the only question left is do we have a Democrat in Washington with the guts to step up to the plate and initiate this committee—i.e., pull back the curtain so that the American people can see the Republican's real agenda?

Jim Green, Democrat candidate for Congress, 2000
www.Inclusivism.org

President Obama/Fellow Democrats--

There is a famous line from F. Scott Fitzgerald's "The Great Gatsby" regarding the carelessness of Tom and Daisy---a wealthy couple—and I'll paraphrase--they "smash up things and then retreat back into their money, leaving it to others to clean up their mess"

Is this not the quintessential definition of the Republican Party over the past 30 years?

U.S. Representative Ron Paul, a doctrinaire Libertarian—in an interview on CNN 4-21-11-- was more pointed when he asserted that we played right into bin Laden's hand—squandering our wealth in America on Iraq and Afghanistan, etc.—and bringing our economy to the brink of collapse—finished bin Laden's attack on 9-11-

And whether bin Laden could actually read us that well--— Congressman Paul was dead-on correct with the end result—

Further, our economic collapse in 1987 should have served as fair warning that Supply-Side Economics has a shelf-life of only about 7 years before the economy starts caving in on itself—

We can't siphon America's wealth away from the consuming middle—the 98% of us [by giving obscene tax cuts for the top 2%] without sending our economy into a tailspin!

But by not learning from this lesson, we had to relive it again in 2008—only this time it created the worst economic disaster since the Great Depression!

And in the greatest shift upward of wealth in our history at present—400 persons now hold more of American's wealth than 150 million of the rest of us do!

Further, we need to remind the Republicans in the Senate and House who espouse, daily, that cutting taxes for the 2% will solve our unemployment crisis [the Republican's One and Only job creation solution]—That this is what we are doing NOW—[the tax cuts were extended] and it has left us with 14 million Americans still unemployed!

And finally, how anyone could buy into Congressman Paul Ryan's deficit reduction plan—Supply-Side Economics on steroids—is beyond human comprehension!

Jim Green, Democrat candidate for Congress, 2000
www.Inclusivism.org

F. Michael Kelleher, Special Assistant to the President

President Obama/Fellow Democrats.

Only 20% of Americans have the "deficit" as their highest priority for Congress to fix—while according to a recent Zogby poll "86% of Americans think the government should provide a job to anyone who wants one".

In short, Job Creation is overwhelmingly more important to the American people, at present, than the deficit—and yet, *all* of the political focus in Washington has shifted from our unemployment crisis [with almost 14 million Americans still unemployed] --to the "deficit"—

Which should cause all of us to question, and perhaps with more than a little alarm. When did this happen, and why did this happen?

And the "When" appears to have two parents. when the 2010 election brought in a wrath of radical Republicans [AKA Tea Party] –with an anti-government "starve the beast" mind-set—and when President Obama appointed a "deficit commission" rather than a "job creation commission"—[perhaps, believing HR 2847 was a solution—when, in fact, it has been a miserable failure!].

It was a decision Democrats would live to regret—given the mandate by the American people in 2008. Fix Unemployment! Had we fixed unemployment--every bill passed by we Democrats, including healthcare reform, would have been bullet-proof—but when we didn't, everything we did became a target.

With the end result that we got hammered in the 2010 election—and a "radical" plan [Ryan] which would destroy Medicare Insurance—and the "Big Lie" according to Eliot Spitzer, by the Republicans in Congress, that "cutting marginal [tax] rates for those at the top will create jobs" [when THIS IS WHAT WE ARE DOING NOW—the tax cuts were extended!]--

To put in perspective. We have 20 years, and hard work, to fix the deficit—but we have 5 minutes to fix our unemployment crisis—As Harry Hopkins noted in the 30's "People don't eat some day, they eat every day"!

So how do we Democrats wrest America back from this dangerous sabotage—and re-set the agenda to what Americans want us to focus on. Job Creation?

A good start would be for the administration to get behind Rep Conyers' 21st Century Humphrey Hawkins Bill, currently in committee in the House.

Jim Green, Democrat candidate for Congress, 2000

www.Inclusivism.org

President Obama/Fellow Democrats:

When on earth did our policy makers get locked into the notion that our "only" source of jobs in America is from the "private sector"? Or that this is even the best source of jobs—it is a sacred cow that, at present, has locked 14 million Americans out of a job!

When every waking moment in capitalism is spent pondering ways to eliminate as many of us humans, as possible, from the workforce—to increase "profits"—Why on earth would we look to this model to solve our unemployment crisis in America?

It would be ideal if the market would absorb everyone in—but it never has, and it never will!

Further, this "sacred cow" injures capitalism, as well as the unemployed! The market thrives when we have a robust, employed, consuming workforce!

We have a lot of definitions of what "The American Dream" means—mine is, "Make a better paperclip, sell it for a million bucks, and retire in south Florida"— so notions that this is an anti-capitalism tyrant is sheer poppycock!

It is our "sacred cow"—that jobs can only come from the private sector--that is anti-capitalism!

And this sacred cow is also the reason why our policy makers embrace the bizarre notion—and have committed hundreds of billions of the taxpayers money to this folly----that "small business" will fix our unemployment crisis!

It would be impossible to have 14 million Americans [almost 1 in 10 of our workforce] still unemployed—if these laws actually worked!

It is clearly plausible that public and private sector jobs can work in concert—indeed, embracing pubic sector employment will create more private sector jobs in 6 months, than HR 2847 [The HIRE ACT] in 6 years—so what is our aversion to public sector jobs?

This is not suggesting that public sector jobs would be employed by the federal government, but rather that a fund would be created to fund the millions of jobs, in every jurisdiction in America that every year go unfilled, for lack of funding—See: www.Inclusivism.org

The fact is, we have far more jobs that need to be done in America—than persons to fill these jobs—so public sector jobs are a "win-win"—the American people win, and capitalism wins!

It is currently projected by the IMF that China is going to pass up the American economy in 2016—while we cling to our "sacred cow" to the last burning ember--

The world has changed, our solutions haven't, and the result for America--is disastrous--

Jim Green, Democrat candidate for Congress, 2000

President Obama/Fellow Democrats.

I cannot help but think that the biting criticism of President Obama—by Princeton Professor Cornel West—relates to the golden opportunity the Obama administration/Democrats had to end pervasive unemployment in America—and particularly as this adversely impacts minorities—and the Obama administration let this golden opportunity slip by and is now stuck with a window that may well be closed.

At the beginning of the Obama administration the American public extended an open hand and was expecting and welcomed "bold experimentation"—we wanted results and were convinced the Obama administration could produce results. And if we recall, Americans were saying "Fix Unemployment" long before the Bush meltdown infinitely compounded the problem.

But the administration got bad advice—and locked into a mind-set that "private sector jobs" could end our unemployment crisis—it would be ideal if the market would provide everyone with a job—but the empirical evidence is indisputable—"private sector jobs" can never more than make a dent in our unemployment—and a tiny dent at that—and if the data from Fareed Zakaria is correct we still have 25 million Americans without work—two years down our current path—in sum, the world has changed, our solutions haven't, and result has been disastrous--

It is impossible to say we are on the right path if we have 25 million Americans still unemployed, and sadly the open hand at the beginning became a closed fist in the 2010 election—when our unemployment had barely ticked downward—and at $2.5 million for every private sector job created--our current path became a cost-effective nightmare.

The public interchanges the words "economy" and "unemployment" and even in our modest recovery the public perception is that our economy is doing poorly, and rates the Obama administration accordingly on the economy—because we did not fix unemployment.

In the alternative, if at the beginning--the administration would have acted on the authority under Humphrey-Hawkins to create a "reservoir of public employment" –with the target provided in this law to reduce unemployment to "3%"—all of the good works by the Obama administration since –would have been bullet-proof, rather than—as it has turned out—including the disappointment of Professor West—a target—

There is a maxim "It is never too late to do the right thing" and Representative Conyers has introduced a latter-day Humphrey-Hawkins Bill – HR 870 [currently in Committee in the House]—

and we fund without adding a dime to our deficit. See also:
www.Inclusivism.org

Jim Green, Democrat candidate for Congress, 2000

President Obama/Fellow Democrats،

Ending our unemployment crisis in America is comparable to getting bin Laden, to the 10th power--

The Obama administration has a real shot at ending our unemployment crisis in America by getting behind HR 870, introduced by Congressman Conyers [currently in Committee]—

And "0" chance by staying on our current path—with HR 2847 costing the taxpayers $2.5 million per each $9 per hour "private sector job" created—and virtually no change in our unemployment rate--

A large part of the problem is that we have been duped by right-wing propaganda—that has sabotaged an effective solution, and the American people—more on this shortly--

Gore Vidal asserts America is amnesic re our history--and we need to recall that unemployment was the number one political issue in America—Before the Bush economic meltdown took the problem into a whole new orbit—

The truth is, the problem is systemic, and calls for a systemic solution—the world has changed, our solutions haven't, and as a result--the path we are currently following has been disastrous!

We need to mark the source of our current unemployment crisis back to around 1975, give or take—when the colliding forces of globalization, automation, etc., reached a critical mass—resulting in ubiquitous unemployment—in short, we became victims of our progress--

Our response to the malaise in the 70's, caused by pervasive unemployment in America, was the Humphrey-Hawkins Full Employment Act, in 1978 [hereafter H-H].

Specifically, this law authorizes the government to create a "reservoir of public employees"—any time our unemployment rises above "3%" – i.e., it is a Pro-Market solution that can be funded without adding a dime to our deficit. i.e., two examples, HR 870/ www.Inclusivism.org

To undermine H-H, in 1979, a wealthy ultra-right foundation funded a fraudulent study by a student at MIT [with no background in economics]—which asserted that "small business private sector jobs" would provide all the jobs needed in America—[to sabotage a government role in fixing our pervasive unemployment] and the foundation then spent millions of dollars promoting this fraudulent concept!

Our proof that this concept doesn't work. It would be impossible to have 14-25 million Americans still unemployed if this flawed study was correct—because we bought into it hook, line and sinker—it is the premise we are foolishly following at present to fix our unemployment crisis--

Jim Green, Democrat candidate for Congress, 2000

RE: Press conference 7/11/11

President Obama/Fellow Democrats:

WHY ON GOD'S EARTH WOULD SOCIAL SECURITY INSURANCE
BE A PART OF THE DEFICITS CAUSED BY IRRESPONSIBLE AND
RECKLESS REPUBLICAN POLICIES OF THE PAST 30 YEARS?

Why on earth would we put a self-sustaining Insurance
program—[Social Security] that brings in more money than it
pays out—be "on the table"?

It has nothing to do with the "deficit"—and those who complain
about paying interest on the moneys stolen from the Social
Security Trust Fund—or somehow link this to our current deficit
problem—should be incarcerated for Fraud and Theft!

There is an argument for long-term restructuring so that Social
Security Insurance is sustainable after 2037—an actuarial
restructuring common to all insurance—but to say that we just
must do this before August 2, 2011 is patently insane!

Medicare is also an INSURANCE program. As a senior I pay
almost $100 a month for Medicare—I am 77 and so far the
government is ahead of the game—but the problem with

Medicare Insurance is much different than our actuarial problem in 2037.

Medicare Insurance has both long and short-term problems because of waste, fraud and "for profit" profiteers robbing it blind! I am a capitalist—I totally support build a better widget, sell it for a million bucks, and retire in South Florida—but making a "profit" from the healthcare of another human should be a criminal offense!

Finally, why is the word "entitlement" being thrown around like a drunken sailor when referring to the Social Security and Medicare INSURANCE programs? "Entitlement" was invented by wing-nuts in the 1970's—to be derisive—to suggest that these INSURANCE programs are giveaway programs of some kind—do we refer to our auto insurance as an "entitlement"?

Every time anyone in our government or media refers to Social Security and Medicare INSURANCE as an "entitlement" they are deferring to our wing-nuts—to our lowest common denominator—our scumbags, to be frank—persons who are NOT committed to building a safe and sane America in which to live and raise our children—

President Obama. Our constitution mandates that Congress MUST pay our "Debts"—it is not an either/or--The Republicans caused this debt and are now trying to renege on payment and to hold the American people hostage so they can undermine Social Security and Medicare—and you can end this circus via Executive Order—on behalf of the American people--

Jim Green, Democrat candidate for Congress, 2000
www.Inclusivism.org

ATTN: Austan Goolsby – The White House

With all due respect to the road metaphor--rather than an
innocuous "bump in the road" sign, it should read "bridge out
ahead" as a warning to us Democrats that we are on the wrong
road to solve our unemployment crisis in America—

When we have 14-25 million Americans still unemployed
[depending on economist] it is impossible to disregard that the
world has changed, our solutions haven't, and the result has been
disastrous--

—It is the "opinion" of "conventional wisdom" that the best way to
fix our unemployment crisis—is with "private sector jobs"— and
cling to this notion like a ticket on the Titanic -- insisting we are
on the right road—

And as a result we have crafted our legislation– and committed
billions of the taxpayers dollars around this erroneous concept --
to make this opinion come true—

But the bottom line is: What We Are Doing Isn't Working!

Another component of this—the public sees as synonymous and
inter-changeable terms "economy" and "employment"— and
which the Republicans are more than happy to exploit—

For instance, when Romney declares President Obama has done a miserable job with the economy [even though it was a masterful job on one level]—the public agrees with Romney—because we have not fixed our unemployment crisis—and in spite of the fact that Bush's economic meltdown made the problem infinitely worse—

Our unemployment dilemma dates to the mid-70's, and the Humphrey-Hawkins Full Employment Act [15 USC § 3101] signed into law by President Carter, correctly assesses the solution essential in a modern economy—a solution that is both pro-market, and addresses the social crisis caused by unemployment.

Specifically, the government/president is "authorized" to create a "reservoir of public employment"—at any time out unemployment rate exceeds "3%"—[and we are three times over the percent necessary to trigger this law]—Additionally, Rep. Conyers has picked up the banner with HR 870 [currently in Committee]—and it is inexplicable why it is being disregarded—

Further, there are various deficit-neutral methods to fund a public workforce, please see: HR 870 – www.Inclusivism.org

Will the Republicans try to undermine – is the Pope a Catholic – but the public wants to chip in and supports a Neighbor-To-

Neighbor Job Creation Act—and the Republicans need to exposed for opposing job creation—

This is a "win-win" solution—the American people win, and capitalism wins—

Jim Green, Democrat candidate for Congress, 2000

President Obama/Fellow Democrats:

On June 13, 2011—Larry Summers, President Obama's first, and former, Director of the National Economic Council, projected that our unemployment rate should be down to 8% before the 2012 election—

Based on this projection we can definitively say that as an advisor on "unemployment"—[and in particular during the Great Recession]—President Obama could have gotten worse advice from his top economic advisor—but it is difficult to see how—

Professor Summers was brilliant in understanding the fix re our investment banking, but horrible in his understanding the cause and results of unemployment--And we have 24 million Americans unemployed or underemployed as proof!

There is no rational explanation why our unemployment rate in America, today, should exceed 3%—None—

Had Director Summers [our "conventional wisdom"] actually understood this social/economic/political problem and how to solve it—

We would have had legislation in the hopper and/or enforced existing legislation [15 USC § 3101]-- within the first 90 days, and we Americans would have been well on our way to 3% unemployment by the end of 2009—

Further, had this been the case, the American people, currently, would be considering an amendment to our Constitution so that President Obama could serve more than two terms—rather than seriously considering limiting to one—

To illustrate, we would never condemn the CEO for closing a plant, if they are losing money—but the American people are outraged by a government that lacks the imagination and wherewithal to step up to the plate with a solution to this lapse in our market system—

And at present we are asking the market to fix itself with both hands tied behind its back—by inexplicably, looking upon government involvement as if it were the plague, and insisting upon solving our unemployment crisis with "private sector jobs"—a concept that is antithetical to capitalism!

Full Employment is a Pro-Market concept—the market thrives when we have a robust, employed, consuming public – and we have far more jobs that need to be done in America, in every jurisdiction in America, than we have persons to fill these jobs—

While America drowns in myths and sacred cows-

The bottom line is, HR 870 [currently in Committee] can fix our unemployment crisis without adding a dime to our deficit, see also: www.Inclusivism.org –and are "win-win" solutions—the American people win, and capitalism wins!

Jim Green, Democrat candidate for Congress, 2000

PUTTING "COOL" BACK IN THE OBAMA CAMPAIGN.

In the public's mind the words "economy" and "employment" [and in this case "unemployment"] mean one and the same thing—i.e., the Republicans are on to this and are using the word "economy" as code to be derisive towards President Obama—given our horrid 9.1% unemployment rate—

And the handlers saying that we Democrats get an "A" for effort re fixing our unemployment crisis—NO—the public wants RESULTS—and they said this in no uncertain terms during the 2010 election—

The over-arching question re unemployment has turned on "private sector jobs" vs "public sector jobs"—and the administration has gotten bad advice—i.e., it is impossible to say we are on the right path to create private sector jobs when we still have 24 million unemployed/ underemployed in America!

The bottom line is, HR 2847 The HIRE Act [warmed over Reaganomics]—IS NOT WORKING—the result is the PROOF!

David Stockman [a Democrat at heart], former director of OMB [expressing the the Republican mind-set]—even he has on blinders and can see the funding to create jobs as only coming from borrowed money---Really? Where is their Yankee Ingenuity? Where is their imagination?

Capitalism prospers when we have a robust, employed, consuming public—the Republicans say that corporations are not hiring from the $2 trillion in cash they are sitting on—because of Democrat policies—BS—they are not hiring because they need consumers of their products—and we have almost 1 in 10 Americans idle!

Humphrey-Hawkins [15 USC § 3101 - hereafter H-H] is dead-on correct—When our unemployment rises above "3%" our government has an absolute obligation to step up to the plate and create a "reservoir of public employees". We have far more jobs that need to be done, in every jurisdiction in America, than we have persons to fill these jobs--

And, by the government not creating public sector jobs we are asking capitalism to fix our economy, and itself, with both hands tied behind its back—

And rather than throwing our hands up in despair re funding the public sector jobs mandated under H-H—there are numerous methods that will not add a dime to our deficit, or require our borrowing the money—

Rep. Conyers has a Bill in Committee [HR 870] asking Wall Street to fund, and our employed chipping in to help their neighbor [www.Inclusivism.org], to name only two—and we can end our unemployment crisis in 6 months, not 6 years—and stimulate our economy in the process--now that is "COOL"--

Jim Green, Democrat candidate for Congress, 2000

REPUBLICANS, THE TAX CUTS WERE EXTENDED—WHERE ARE
THE JOBS?

President Obama/Fellow Democrats:

The reason we still have 9.2% unemployment is because those
delegated to fix the problem—good intentions accepted—didn't
know how to fix the problem---

The truth is--the world has changed, our solutions haven't, and
the result has been disastrous—

We fail to fix our unemployment crisis because:

1] We fail to see that unemployment is a "social" problem—
capitalism is in the "for profit" business, not in the "solving social
problems" business—and when every waking moment in
capitalism is spent pondering ways to eliminate as many of us
humans, as possible, from the workplace to increase "profits"—it
defies rational human thought why we would count on [let alone
exclusively] "private sector jobs" to solve this "social" problem?
The primary role of government is to solve "social" problems--

2] We still have on foot on the plantation—the mind-set which frames our policies looks upon humans as entities to be "used and discarded at will"—

3] We failed to account for the "innovation syndrome". We celebrate innovation—but rapidly develop a "deer in the headlights" look re what to do with the 9 persons displaced by the innovation—and the same syndrome applies to automation, globalization, etc. –the Republican solution is to pretend the problem doesn't exist, or admonishes the employee to brush up their resume—

4] We failed to account for how we got where were at— somewhere around the mid-1970's the colliding mega-forces, innovation, technology, automation, globalization, etc., reached a critical mass resulting in ubiquitous unemployment in all of the OECD countries, the US included—and we have been befuddled ever since with what to do with the displaced employee—And the Republican drivel that cutting taxes will create jobs need to be reminded –THE TAX CUTS WERE EXTENDED—WHERE ARE THE JOBS?

5] We fail to recognize that Humphrey-Hawkins [signed by President Carter in 1978] IS the answer—[see also HR 870, currently in Committee]—Specifically, the government has a solemn responsibility to create a "reservoir of public employees—

[the "generic job" if you will]" anytime our unemployment rises above "3%"—and we are 3 times over this % at present—

A proposed Senate Bill is The Neighbor-To-Neighbor Job Creation Act. A federally mandated, mutual insurance, owned by our employed—to provide a fund to hire/train our unemployed. Re. www.Inclusivism.org

Jim Green, Democrat candidate for Congress, 2000

F. Michael Kelleher, Special Assistant to the President.

President Obama/Fellow Democrats.

WHY IS HR 870 BEING IGNORED?

It is understandable why we used the TARP and Stimulus tens of billions to swab up the mess caused by Wall Street—to prevent the American economy from going off a cliff—

But we dropped the ball when we did not fix our unemployment crisis--integral to a comprehensive solution—and we are now paying the price—

It is impossible for us to have 9.2% unemployment, and conclude that "conventional wisdom" got right re how to fix our unemployment crisis—

Indeed, we should have put fixing unemployment ahead of fixing Wall Street, in our priorities—because the market thrives when we have a robust, employed, consuming public—and the noted $2 trillion our corporations are sitting on is because they do not have consumers buying their products—

Capitalism is not in the "solving social problems" business [if they want to stay in business]—that is why we don't see them rushing

out to hire millions of people [which puzzles our idealists]—
when they don't have consumers for their products—

A metaphor re our economic meltdown is a three-legged stool—
the Wall Street meltdown, the housing meltdown [with the first
two integral to each other], and the employment meltdown—

With the bottom line—had we fixed unemployment, this in kind
would have fixed the other two—or conversely. Until we get
serious about a WORKABLE SOLUTION for our unemployment
crisis—we can forget finding a substantive solution to the Great
Recession—

We have a lot of baggage standing in the way of our finding a
WORKABLE SOLUTION, including some certifiable members of
Congress, nevertheless--

U.S. Representative Conyers has introduced legislation to fix our
unemployment crisis, and the only viable solution on our radar.
HR 870 [currently in Committee], a latter-day Humphrey
Hawkins Full Employment Act [15 USC § 3101, hereafter H-H].

Specifically, H-H authorizes the government/president to create a
"reservoir of public employees" anytime our unemployment goes
above "3%"—and we can fund without adding a dime to our
deficit under HR 870, see also. www.Inclusivism.org

HR 870 is a Pro-Market, "win-win solution"—capitalism wins, and the American people win—So the minute following President Obama signing an Executive Order ending our debt ceiling crisis [if it comes to that] our next question should be, WHY IS HR 870 BEING IGNORED?

Jim Green, Democrat candidate for Congress, 2000

CHAPTER TWO, Fail-Safe Electronic Voting

So long as the potential for manipulation of electronic voting continues to exist—our elections in America will be in peril! In spite of all the polls showing a strong Obama victory--it was not until 10PM Central on 11-4-08.....that we could breath a sigh of relief....we had been cheated out of the past two elections....with many believing that Bush was never legally elected president of the United States....and we were braced for the worst.......this can, and MUST be fixed before 2010, so that this never happens again, and in the interest of all who support fair and open elections-- regardless of party. Accordingly, it is urged that we adopt the following proposed "FAIL-SAFE ELECTRONIC VOTING ACT".

THE FAIL-SAFE ELECTRONIC VOTING ACT

1) EVERY electronic voting machine (hereafter EVM), must be inexpensive, identical throughout the U.S. in a 1/150 ratio, and *must count and produce a hard-copy of the recorded votes.* In addition, an extra copy of their recorded votes would be produced (not necessarily a hard-copy), marked "Voter's Copy", and containing "NOTICE. Do Not Destroy Until Every Election On Your Ballot Is Certified". [If Wal-Mart refused to give us a receipt for our purchases—would they not be suspect—and this regards our democracy].

2) *After confirming that their votes are recorded correctly,* the voter would then insert the hard-copy ballot into a software-free (count only) optical scanner (hereafter OS), for a second count. The hard-copy ballot would be retained by election officials in the

event a candidate asks for a recount (*not possible under the current system, and which undermines the legality of each such election).* The EVM and the OS must be manufactured by different companies (which is universally true today).

3) Election officials assigned to oversee the EVM, would be prevented by law from overseeing the OS, and vice-versa, and stiff criminal penalties would be imposed for violations.

4) Further, every EVM would be programmed with raw data re the total registration rolls, by party, and norms for their voting history, etc.,----as an "alert" to a possible irregularity, such as an "Under-vote"—or "vote-flipping" etc., and *standards* established to suspend certification where there is an "improbable result", at least temporarily, of a particular election until the discrepancy is cleared up. (This is what computers do best, and it would be very easy to create such a program).

5) At the end of the election day, tallies would be taken from the EVM and the OS, for each candidate. *If the tallies didn't balance for any given election, or if there is an "alert", that election cannot be certified until the "error" is corrected.* If the candidates agree (the victory is certain), minor discrepancies in the count could be disregarded. While probably rare, the Voter, or a random sample of Voters, would be required by law to return their Copy of the

recorded votes to the election office to clear up any "error", or where an "alert" signals the need for same.

6) Further, every state provides for a recount when the total vote falls below a certain percent of difference between the candidates, impossible to conduct with the current EVM—and thus Congress must mandate the following regarding presidential candidates. A RUN-OFF election is mandated and triggered in those states where the percent of total vote is less than .5% of difference between any given candidates; said election to be held on the second Saturday following the election, on PAPER BALLOTS ONLY, and contain ONLY the names of the relevant candidates, for instance. "Barack Obama, Democrat" and "John McCain, Republican"—with oversight in counting by a representative(s) of each party—said procedure providing more than adequate time to meet the Electoral College mandate. NOTE. Had this been the law in 2000, Al Gore would be our president, and the American economy would not be in meltdown!

7) Finally, absent the above safeguards, and until these safeguards are in place—Congress must mandate that PAPER BALLOTS, ONLY, can be used in our presidential elections. This is not a "partisan" issue, it is a "pro-democracy" issue. Most importantly, this will return the responsibility for our elections, and our vote counting, back into the hands of the individual voter, where it belongs, and out of the hands of "corporate control"---*it is after*

all "our democracy", itself, that is at risk if we don't take these steps---and in that regard, is there any time or cost differential that is too great?

Reply To: Jim Green -- Democrat candidate for Congress, Dist 21, TX, 2000

jgreen5@satx.rr.com   www.Inclusivism.org

AMENDED/UPDATED:------->The best intentions in the world for the changes the vast majority of Americans agree we need to make--are meaningless, in the absence of fair and honest elections—

PROPOSED PLANK IN THE 2008 DEMOCRATIC NATIONAL PLATFORM

SUBJECT: Election Reform: The "Help America Vote Act" (HAVA), passed by Congress in 2002, has become the Help Republicans Win Act....due to a lack of over-sight of the "private for Profit" corporations that built our Electronic Voting Machines, and then claimed corporate ownership of the software for counting our votes. The Democrat Party supports fair and open elections, and to that end will insist that Congress pass "The Fail-Safe Voting Act", herein above, to protect the integrity of the voting rights of each individual citizen.

President Obama/Fellow Democrats,

A manufacturing job we should start tomorrow is creating a fail-safe electronic machine—or rather system—and have in place by the November election.

Given the known problems with computer security—our democracy is at risk at present, and include "vote-flipping", "under-votes", as well as other deceptions.

Further, there are millions of unspent dollars from HAVA, passed in 2002, and additional funding may not be necessary.

To be viable, a Fail-Safe Electronic Voting System would include:

1] a relatively inexpensive electronic voting machine [hereafter EVM]that would produce a hard copy of the votes we cast, as well as a copy to be retained by the voter and marked "Voter's Copy"—with the votes cast stored on a hard-drive.

2] *After confirming that their votes are recorded correctly,* the voter would then insert the hard-copy ballot into a software-free (count only) optical scanner (hereafter OS), for a second count.

3] At the end of the election day, tallies would be taken from the EVM and the OS, for each candidate. *If the tallies didn't balance for any given election--that election would not be certified unless the "discrepancy" is corrected.*

In many ways, it is inexplicable why it is not mandatory that every voter receive a "Voter's Copy" today, as their receipt—if Wal-Mart handed us a piece of paper with "trust us"—as a receipt for our purchases—we would be outraged, and, here, it is our democracy at risk!

Further, the hard-copy ballot would be retained by election officials in the event a candidate asks for a recount (*not possible under the current system, and which undermines the legality of each such election*).

Election officials assigned to oversee the EVM, would be prevented by law from overseeing the OS, and vice-versa, and stiff criminal penalties would be imposed for violations.

Further, every EVM would be programmed with voting norms as an "alert" to a possible "under-vote" or "vote-flipping" etc., and *standards* established to suspend certification where there is an "improbable result"—[This is what computers do best, and it would be very easy to create such a program].

Finally, in submitting bids we need to look with a jaundiced eye at the bidder. Also, with no government oversight per the FEC—and the Republican "Voter ID" hysteria, with poll-tax fingerprints all over it---and both as a distraction from EVM fraud.....

....what we have now is a nightmare, and our democracy at risk!

Jim Green, Democrat candidate for Congress, 2000

CHAPTER THREE. Miscellaneous -- Self- Explanatory sent mostly via Facebook

RE. the role of government--Republican policy for the past 30 years, and to this day, is to siphon America's wealth away from the consuming middle—and give it to the already wealthy]via obscene tax cuts—and driving up our deficit]—which has a shelf-life of about 7 years before the economy collapses [1987 & 2008]—In short, anyone voting for Republicans to run our government—is Brain-Dead www.Inclusivism.org

---

Zakaria had opined on his CNN program GPS, that Paul Ryan was "brave" in his corrupt proposed budget cuts which caused this critical response. And question why our media is not honest about Ryan and his ilk---these are "Not Decent People"! Neither is Limbaugh, or most of the Republicans in Congress—their single objective is to pander to the GREED of their wealthiest contributors—NOT what is in the best interest of the great majority of American, or America!

Fareed Zakaria. You are confusing "brave" with "hypocrisy" in your observation of Ryan's despicable deficit reduction plan. It is very important for us out here in the hinterland to get accurate information [at least some of us]—i.e., "no spin" information from persons we can trust to be accurate—And, unfortunately that took you down a couple of notches because it is Reaganomics— the worst crime ever perpetrated on the American people--on steroids! Among other things, Reaganomics has a shelf-life of about 7 years before the economy starts collapsing in on itself [1987 & 2008]—we can't siphon America's wealth away from the consuming middle without sending our economy into a tailspin, and compounded by increasing the deficit to make up the shortfall in revenue! In short, Ryan's plan would create an America unfit for human habitation—and under no circumstances could it be described as "brave"!

Jim Green, Democrat candidate for Congress, 2000
www.Inclusivism.org

Every one of our economic theories relates to only one species— US, us human beings—and yet not a single theory recognizes the right of us humans to work and be a productive citizen—the most fundamental of our human needs—

Rather, with few exceptions our economic theories are about the "almighty dollar"—and what the almighty dollar can do to make our rich, richer—

In short, us humans are an extraneous footnote—to be used and discarded at will—but always with the end in mind of making the rich, richer—

From Australia, we do have the Buffer Stock Employment Model—which urges an expanding and contracting public workforce—which expands during downturns in the market, and contracts as the market recovers—

THE PSYCHOLOGICAL IMPACT OF UNEMPLOYMENT

The 9.2 unemployment rate is greater than the loss of income for those unemployed. The Zeitgeist is a malaise on the part of the public, and loss of confidence in our economy—in spite of our modest recovery.

RE₁ the Republican Primaries/Agenda₁ Turning America back over to the Republicans could be compared to handing the keys to your new Cadillac to a fallen down drunk--who wrecked it last week--in the hopes they will not wreck it again—Surely, the American people are not that stupid? www.Inclusivism.org

---

RE, Ed Henry [who obviously doesn't have enough to do in Hawaii]--For those who ponder if America is on the skids...finis...on our last leg as a great nation—now have their confirmation when a major network wants to pander to our certified idiots—our "birthers" [giving them even 5 seconds of our time, is 5 seconds too long!]—let's do it this way—even if Obama was born on Mars, his mother was a U.S. citizen—which automatically makes him a U.S. citizen—END OF STORY!

The blather that for everyone to have a job we have to create "make work" jobs—is a myth, propaganda BS, our imagination being drowned by a "sacred cow"—the fact is, we have far more work that needs to be done in America, than we have persons to fill these jobs—We do not have a shortage of jobs, we have a shortage of imagination! The Harvard Boys Club on Amazon

---

It is easy to be glib about creating jobs—Romney does it at every speech—so why doesn't anyone in our media ask him, or his campaign, to explain in unequivocal terms how he plans to do that? Does it include cutting taxes for the 1% [how is it distinguished from Bush II]? It is a legitimate "public's right to know" question—required of a "free press"!

The CBO is projecting that following our current trajectory [our current job creation mind-set] that our unemployment will be reduced to 7% by 2015, and 5.5% by 2017—five years from now--This is sad in two ways—first, that anyone would be OK with this—and secondly, because Romney should change his name from Mitt to Hyperbole Romney, because he is trying to snow the American people with a "pipe dream" by sneaking "W's" job creation scheme in through the back door—which was a miserable failure! And what about the consumers our markets will lose out on if we stay on our current course?

The rank and file would do well to heed the warning by President Truman in 1948—that it is us, the American people, who will be the "loser" if we fail to inform ourselves and return America to "VooDoo Economics"!

Many mark America as going off the rails when Bush II was appointed to the presidency—but where America actually went off the rails is when they failed to elect Vice-President Hubert Humphrey to the presidency, in 1968. Humphrey was spot-on correct in his ACCURATE perception of how the world has changed—and what was ESSENTIAL to address these changes. We can go on endlessly in an esoteric discussion, or even emotion/politically driven discussion [and central to this election], about what is—or isn't a "free-enterprise" system—but if we don't get the basics correct—if we don't accurately perceive the problem and how to fix it—we get it wrong, and it would be impossible to have an 8.1% if we got it right....

In a nutshell, with the Republican debates as Exhibit I, re the national Republican agenda this year—If their lips are moving—they are either lying, or they are a hypocrite—and they are counting on the rank and file who vote Republican to have amnesia!

Senator Udall--RE. Newsletter "Winning the Global Economic Race"—3-2-11—until we fix unemployment, all else we do is irrelevant!

Show me a "birther"—I'll show you a "racist"—So why don't we tell the truth—that Trump is trying to incite the ignorant underbelly in America—what is worst about America—rather than what is best about America? See. The Harvard Boys Club on Amazon www.Inclusivism.org

---

President Obama had a weapon not available to FDR in the war against an economy that had melted away in sheer terror. The Social Security and Military Retirement moneys percolating up through our economy, which not only contributed to Bill Gates becoming the wealthiest man in the world—were it not for these money [Social Security did not start trickling into our economy until 1940]—but were it not for these moneys we would not be talking about having narrowly averted another Great Depression in 2008—We would be buried in one....

ANTHOLOGY III

AMERICA IS ONE SICK MF: Why Greed-Driven America Went
Off The Rails....

DEDICATED TO:
Those dedicated to fixing it....

PROLOGUE

We have elements in America that will say that I "hate" America
for making that statement—but they would be dead-wrong—

Indeed, it is their ignorance of America--that has America so
FU—We cannot start fixing what is wrong with America, until
we start fessing-up to what we are doing wrong—And when we
cannot tell the truth in a "free" country—it is no longer a "free"
country....Further, the following are "institutional flaws" that call
for the American people to step up—and getting rid of the
current crop of Republicans: governors, in our state houses, and
in Washington, would be a good start....

In the governor race in Texas in 1994, Governor Ann Richards
remarked in response to a concern for the explosion of prison

building in Texas at the time "If you violate the law in Texas, we have a place to lock you up."

The remark didn't help Governor Richards to get re-elected [she lost to W]—and in spite of her prison reforms—the statement was to appease an electorate [suffering from intense feelings of low self-esteem—more on the political implications of this epidemic later] that had taken a sharp turn to the right—and straight into bananaville—[which has metastasized—and gotten even more widespread and rigid in the years since—and includes a racism vote in this election].

For instance, we are six weeks out from the 2012 election [we will probably know the result by the time this is published]—but given the destructive, almost fatal damage done to America when W was appointed to the presidency—this election should not even be close and President Obama should win it hands down [at least by 20 points--and he may yet] but as I write it is neck-and-neck—Impossible if we had an informed and rational electorate—and suffering from severe amnesia!

So where is the evidence that "America is one sick MF"? Consider this.

We have the same prison population as China—but they have a billion more people! No other civilized country in the world even comes close to our incarceration rate—and our PR is that we are the most free? We have 5% of the world's population, and 25% of all prison inmates on earth—in our prisons! And since 1990 it has also in many states become a privatized "for profit" criminal industry!

Further, 70% of our prison population are in for "non-violent" offenses, and we daily turn non-violent offenders into violent career criminals—even disregarding the destruction to our family units--by our insane incarceration rate!

We pay twice as much for healthcare in America, for half the result [only a slight exaggeration]—than any other industrial country in the world—and this is for only one reason: PURE GREED!

We have a tiny handful of "profiteers"—who don't even so much as put a Band-Aid on a patient—who annually siphon billions of dollars out of our healthcare system for their own personal aggrandizement and GREEDY self-interests—leaving 44,000 American to die every year due to the high costs of healthcare—and their GREED has relegated America to 37th in the world in healthcare, according to the World Health Organization!

And GREED is so pervasive in our healthcare system that it has become a magnet for persons who see it as a way to get rich, rather than the time-honored goal of medicine—to cure the ill.

And when we look at our gun violence in America, we need to ask. Why do we have this unconscionable gun violence? The sheer numbers of homicides by handguns, alone, tells the whole story. Canada 151, Australia 57, Germany 373, Japan 19, England and Wales 54, the United States 11,789 [numbers which remain relatively static year after year]! And, when we add in all deaths by guns, including the fact that 9 children are killed by guns everyday in America, our gun violence escalates to a staggering 28,663!

As one astute observer noted, "The drug war is over—we lost"— and while we claim that by criminalizing drugs we are keeping them out of the hands of our youth, but as every middle school student knows—it is 10 times easier to get pot, than alcohol, because it is regulated by the state.

Further, half of the persons we have in our prisons are in for drug-related offenses [either directly or indirectly]—

Our war on drugs is a "lose-lose-lose proposition: the loss of tens of billions to maintain our prisons, the loss of dollars to educate our youth [which are competing for the same tax dollars], and the loss in tax revenue by our not decriminalizing drugs—even disregarding the health and hemp benefits of pot!

But the mother of all shortcomings in America, is our unemployment crisis—which existed before Bush II made it infinitely worse—but persists because we still have one foot on the plantation—and insist that it is only the "market" that can create jobs!

Unemployment is a "social" problem—and the last place we should look to solve this problem is anything as unstable and erratic as the "market", which only hires people to increase their "profit", not to solve "social" problems—I am a capitalist---I want the market to succeed—but the objectives are distinctly different….and at present we undermine the Market—in the erroneous belief of helping it—more on this below--

For clarity, we should never condemn the CEO who closes a plant because they are losing money, but we should be outraged by a government that is indifferent or inept in addressing the "social" problems caused by this lapse in the market.

This does not mean that the government should create jobs— [frequently misperceived as WPA] but rather, create and enforce laws that will fill this void within the framework of 15 USC § 3101—which "authorizes" the creation of a "reservoir of public employment" at any time our unemployment in America exceeds "3%" [a Pro-Market solution].

For instance, HR 870 currently pending in the House, or the proposed Neighbor-To-Neighbor Job Creation Act. A federally mandated, mutual insurance—owned by our employed to provide a fund to hire/train our unemployed. See also.
www.Inclusivism.org

For a modest policy cost of 4% of salary we can reduce our unemployment to 3%, within one year of passage—and this solution will create more "private sector" jobs in 6 months, than our current legislation [HR 2847, the HIRE Act] in 6 years, if ever! See more detail. MY LETTERS TO PRESIDENT OBAMA, and OUR GREED AND IGNORANCE, on Amazon/Kindle.

IN SUM, regarding all of the above. The world has changed, our solutions haven't, and the result has been a disaster—and many of our current solutions could be compared to pouring gasoline on a fire, to put it out—

A MAJOR step forward in addressing many of the problems, above [including prison reform]—is for "Conventional Wisdom" to reverse our job creation formula—

At present, the formula is to fix the market, and the market will then fix our unemployment crisis, i.e., fixing unemployment is a step-child in the formula [this may have worked in the past, but not now or going forward—more on this shortly]—at present we need to reverse field—and fix unemployment and this will, in turn, fix the market.

By following the former--our unemployment needle has barely ticked downward—and the result has been a disaster, socially, economically, and politically--it will take years to get back to "5%"—far outstripping unemployment benefits—and under that formula—if the market fails, the unemployed are out of luck!

In political terms, if the Obama administration had followed the latter, The Tea Party would be meeting in a phone booth--all of their progress would have been bullet-proof—rather than as it has turned out—a target.

The following chapters are self-explanatory [letters to the editor and other papers]—and offer suggestions about how we got where we are, and outline proposed solutions for the above. As Oscar Wilde averred "The only truly worthless opinion is an unbiased one"—so bias, agreed—but always in the interest in getting at the larger goal—the truth....

The above is the "How" we went off the rails—the "Why" is more illusive—here is my take. We are a "representative" government--we hire politicians to "represent" what is in our best economic interests—

But when we have a block of voters [identified above] who are mumbling to themselves about gays getting married, or whether women should be forced to have children [even if they have been raped]—and vote against the economic interests of their own children by voting Republican--the national Republican Party is then free to pander to the GREED of their wealthiest contributors—AND THIS IS THE SINGULAR GOAL OF THE REPUBLICAN PARTY! They stand for NOTHING else! And all of the solutions, above, are to pander to the interests of the 1%, and at the expense of the 99%!

This phenomenon is the subject of the book "What's The Matter With Kansas?" and asks the question—in a "representative" government—why on earth would anyone in their right mind vote for a politician who doesn't "represent" them [and please don't say only an idiot]?

In short, If one is not a billionaire, and is voting Republican—they need to have their head examined!

This is not about ideology, folks—it is about logic….

Also, this does not need explanation to the two other people who read this book—[and hopefully understands nuance]--but, I love America, otherwise I would not have written the book—and we have some phenomenal accomplishments—We played a major role in defeating Hitler in WW II, we put a man on the Moon, the list goes on and on—but if I had an uncle, that I loved, who went off the rails—and concludes he was born on Krypton, and thought he could fly—and had taken up residence on the neighbor's roof—it would be remiss to look the other way....

Incidentally, I published my first book on my 78th birthday—and have published a book a month since--this is my seventh [and my last]—and not that I write that fast, or well—the materials were all there for the better part of the past 30 years, give or take, gathering dust—it was just a matter of pulling them together in some order—also, don't believe any book should be over 60 pages, plus/minus—i.e., can be read in the crapper--two hours, max--lol]—but it seems best summed up by a very astute observer [wish I could recall their name to give credit] but re the long delay in publishing. Persons who write do so because they have no choice—they become an "author", however, when people start reading what they have written....

Finally, a note to the reader—the papers and letters are not in sequence, and there is some redundancy [please look for the nuggets...Thx--lol]—also, if you are a "typo-wonk"—are more concerned with sentence structure, etc., than content—you probably won't like my writing—and a wayward capital letter, here and there, and appearing out of place and used for emphasis—editorial license—so apologies, here—

Just look for content, please....THX

CHAPTER ONE

THE HISTORY OF HOW WE GOT WHERE WE ARE.

In the mid-1970's, the colliding forces of automation, technology, globalization, etc., reached a critical mass, resulting in ubiquitous unemployment in all of the OECD countries, and has left their leaders conflicted, ever since, regarding the displaced employee—Eurozone unemployment is still in double digits, with Spain at 22.9%, and with high youth unemployment a major factor in Arab Spring.

In the U.S., we took a pro-active role in addressing, and as a direct response to this economic shift—and in 1978 President Carter signed into law 15 USC § 3101--which "authorizes" the creation of a "reservoir of public employment" at any time our unemployment in America exceeds "3%".

The following year, in 1979, however, and in a panic over Humphrey-Hawkins—our ultra-conservative foundations, and desperate to preserve the "market only" job creation concept, embraced a flawed paper by an obscure MIT student, David L. Birch "The Job Generation Process"; and [with lots of cash] gave his paper biblical importance, and every president since has cited his finding as gospel.

Birch's paper concluded that "small businesses" were the greatest generator of new jobs—problem is, for the purposes of policy-making—it is BS. In a study at Harvard University in 2010, "The Myth of Small Business Job Creation" The research shows "no systematic relationship between firm size and growth." And that small businesses can actually detract from job growth—nevertheless, it is still the Republican One and Only job creation solution!

And in spite of this Washington struggles, still, to make this antiquated and unworkable notion, work--that it is only the market that can create jobs—the world has changed, our solutions haven't, and the result has been a disaster, politically as well as otherwise!

It would be impossible to still have 8.3% unemployment if we were on the right path [the result is the proof]—and among other problems with this concept--if the market fails, the unemployed are out of luck [It is the reason Romeny's job creation solution is a farce!].

Further, unemployment is a "social" problem we are seeking to address with a highly unstable, incompatible entity. The Market - -That is, the last place we should look for a reliable solution to our unemployment crisis is The Market....

And, what apparently isn't clear going forward in the 21st Century, is that an expanding and contracting public workforce is an INDISPENSABLE component to the correct functioning of a modern market economy—i.e., The Humphrey-Hawkins Full Employment Act was dead-on correct in 1978—and provided a "win-win" solution for America--

The market thrives when we have a robust, employed, consuming workforce, and it is essential to consumer confidence—and overlooked is that HR 870 [currently in Committee], and the proposed "Neighbor-To-Neighbor Job Creation Act" [hereafter NTN] See: www.Inclusivism.org [both authorized under Humphrey-Hawkins], are deficit-neutral--Pro-Market "win-win" solutions. The American people win, and capitalism wins—

CHAPTER TWO

President Obama/Fellow Democrats:

For the past 65 years we have had two parallel paths to address unemployment in America—

To assure employment for the troops returning from WW II, President Truman signed into law The Full Employment Act of 1946—

This was expanded upon in 1978 with the Humphrey-Hawkins Full Employment Act, signed into law by President Carter—

And a 21st Century version of this path to full employment in America, is pending the House, HR 870.

Humphrey-Hawkins best defines this path to addressing unemployment in America, and it "authorizes" our government to create a "reservoir of public employees" anytime our unemployment rises above "3%".

And in spite of the fact that this path to employment has been the law of the land since 1946—and is a Pro-Market solution [more on this shortly]---Washington has lacked the wherewithal to

implement this path to employment on behalf of the American people—[a point not lost on the "occupy" movement].

Rather, Washington has taken the alternate parallel path—by insisting that human labor is a "component" in the free enterprise system—[barely distinguishable from the machine the human operates] to be used and discarded "at will"—and the Republican propaganda is that it is an attack upon "freedom" to challenge this concept, but whose "freedom"?

As a result, however, "conventional wisdom" has insisted that it is the market, alone, that can fix our unemployment crisis—the result has been a disaster—

The market thrives when we have a robust, employed, consuming public—and by taking this parallel path—we not only have a staggering 8.1% unemployment, but a struggling recovery as well.

Ironically, following WW II, Australia passed a law very similar to our Full Employment Act of 1946—

Difference is—they actually put it into effect—and over the next 30 years—[until the cold winds of conservatism swept in Reagan and Thatcher, etc.] —the government in Australia saw as a solemn responsibility that "anyone willing to work should be provided with a job" [a quote from the "Audacity of Hope"].

The citizens of Australia still refer to this 30 years as their "Golden Age".

Jim Green, Democrat candidate for Congress, 2000
www.Inclusivism.org

CHAPTER THREE

NOTE: In response to Romney's 47% who need to "take
responsibility for their lives"....

Editor/NYTimes:

What is most interesting about Romney saying our troops in
Afghanistan are "freeloaders"—yes folks, our troops, who are
exempt from paying income taxes, are part of that 47% Romney
said are "freeloaders" who don't pay "income taxes"—and need to
"take responsibility for their lives"--

But what is most interesting about Romney's divisive "entitlement"
nonsense—that half the country are "moochers" is that by his
definition--he is talking about almost every rank and file
Republican he is asking to vote for him!

And we need to drill down on in this "mind-set"—exclusive to the
Republican political strategy, today, which is riddled with lies and
half-truths--it is what distinguishes them from Goldwater
Republicans—

Folks, if your child has a lemonade stand—THEY PAY TAXES—
[and are paying at a higher tax rate than Romney/Romeny

propose for themselves]—that is, every person who participates in our economy pays taxes!

The half-truth in the "income tax" PORTION of our paying taxes—is that every working person pays payroll taxes, sales taxes, and most pay property taxes--and with home interest deduction, etc., that PORTION of their paying taxes is exempt!

And an ironic twist in this "freeloaders" nonsense who don't pay any "income tax"—we have 2000 millionaires who, through high paid tax attorneys, etc.—DON'T pay any "income tax"!

But by the Republicans using "income taxes"—this is interpreted by our ignorant and uninformed as "Oh my God, 47% of Americans are on the dole"—AND THAT IS EXACTLY WHAT ROMNEY [the Republicans strategy] WANTS THEM TO BELIEVE! It is a bald-faced lie!

In short, TO DIVIDE US AMERICANS INTO THE "GOOD GUYS VS THE BAD GUYS"—and everyone voting Republican needs to ask if they have become a victim of this obscene tactic?

And, that is the Republican strategy in a nutshell, folks, and they have been feverishly working to perfect it over the past 30 plus years—

We are a "victim" if we are voting against our own economic interests—and the economic interest of our children—

We are a "representative" government, folks—and Romney/Ryan "represents" the rich getting richer [and solely for their personal GREED], and us 99% getting poorer—PERIOD—THEY HAVE NO OTHER PROGRAM!

Finally, if their lips are moving—on FOX, or Limbaugh, etc., etc.,--it is to divide Americans into the "GOOD GUYS VS THE BAD GUYS"—rather than bringing America together in the best interest of Americans, and America!

Jim Green, Democrat candidate for Congress, 2000—See also: MY LETTERS TO PRESIDENT OBAMA, on Amazon/Kindle

CHAPTER FOUR

NOTE: The following is in response to a letter riddled with Republican talking points--in my local paper—it could apply to any city in America....[the names have been changed to protect the guilty]....

Letter to the editor:

Interesting letter from "C E" -- "An economic lesson" on September 9, 2012—I hope he's setting down for my response—

"C" went on a rant, i.e., lecturing about "profit" but fails to mention that more businesses have failed over the past 32 years—as a DIRECT result of Republican policies, and when the Republicans have been in the White House--than in any like period in American history!

Yes, "C"—it is Republican policies that are anti-capitalism—it is their policies that undermine our market economy—and it is long past due to set the record straight regarding the canard that the Republicans are the "pro-business" party—the facts do not support this, excuse the phrase-- "Big Lie"!

We cannot siphon America's wealth away from the consuming middle—and give it to the 1% in obscene tax cuts [GREED JUST

FOR THE SAKE OF GREED—the Republican One and Only agenda]—without sending our economy into a tailspin!

And what a joke—attacking President Obama on "redistribution of wealth"—when this has been bedrock Republican policy since 1980 to redistribute America's wealth to the 1%--and we now have 400 persons who hold more of America's wealth than 150 million of the rest of us!

And as you will recall, "C", as did occur in 1987 [Reagan] and again in 2008 [Bush] —and the American taxpayers were forced to rush in with trillions of dollars to prevent another Great Depression!

Romeny said he would let GM go bankrupt [the Republican solution]—but I'm betting our local GM dealer [our auto industry all across America] will tell you that President Obama got it right!

Surely, "C", you will give credit to President Obama for saving this "for profit" business—and the jobs of a million Americans employed in this industry—won't you?

Actually, I'm glad "C" wrote this letter because it provides the opportunity to expose a whopper by the Republican Party. That "Greed just for the sake of greed [cut taxes for the 1%]" --and "being pro-business" are the same thing---

When IN FACT, they are as different as night and day!

For instance, if cutting taxes for the 1% created jobs [Romney's ONE AND ONLY JOB CREATION SOLUTION], but if this actually worked we would have full employment—BECAUSE THE BUSH TAX CUTS WERE EXTENDED!

And Romney/Ryan wants to cut their taxes, and drive up our deficit up even further—and let's be honest, "C", they want to pick up right where Bush II left off—and we all know how that turned out!

This letter could turn into a book regarding the inaccuracies about our economy in "C's" letter—and in pointing out that if Ryan's lips are moving, he's lying---but time doesn't permit, and will have to saved for another day.

In closing, "C", here is something to chew on—these billionaires you celebrate and who are trying to buy this election---made their billions off of us—the American people—so why do they hide this money in the Cayman Islands, and Swiss bank accounts—to avoid paying taxes and purely for GREED—rather than investing in the betterment of America? Where is their fiduciary obligation to the American people—who made them rich?

Jim Green

CHAPTER FIVE

Memo to Economic Policy Institute:

In my experience, the "consciousness level" for persons regarding rights for the American "employee", in the work place—are all over the map---with some persons being acutely aware of the necessity for employees having rights, and also what those rights might be-----

To others who are oblivious—i.e., draw a blank regarding this subject—and thus chase down blind alleys in looking for solutions to the urgent "social" problem of ubiquitous unemployment—and are blinded to any solution that is not "market" driven [the worst place to look for a viable solution]....

And which almost always start with the fallacy is in believing that we can not fix "unemployment" and the "economy" at the same time—when the correct answer is –of course we can—

But when we are stuck in the mind-set that it is only the "market" that can create jobs—we close our mind to alternative solutions—i.e., alternative solutions are not even on the table—even on the Radar—they are invisible to our "problem solvers"—who, sadly [and perhaps a slight exaggeration], still have one foot on the plantation—

And the myth that "public sector" jobs undermines the "pool of slaves" [the unspoken mind-set] from which "private jobs" are derived, and to be used and discarded "at will" [our current "conventional wisdom"]--

And the proof. For the above to be untrue—HR 870, currently pending in Committee in the House—and which could reduce our unemployment to "3%" within a year of passage—would be front and center—a top priority for our "problem solvers"---

When, in fact, most never even heard of this proposed law—let alone, the public—and there is a blind spot to a major flaw in the "market only" job creation solution. If the market fails, the unemployed are out of luck—

In short, the "market only" approach gives lip service to solving our unemployment crisis—[rather than looking at it as a "stand alone" social problem—independent of he market]—i.e., it is seen as and a step-child in the process—and 8% unemployment is the result—

Jim Green, Democrat candidate for Congress, 2000

CHAPTER SIX

NOTE: Until we fix our Electronic Voting Machine nightmare—
we have little hope in effective change.

So long as the potential for manipulation of electronic voting
continues to exist—our elections in America will be in peril! In
spite of all the polls showing a strong Obama victory--it was not
until 10PM Central on 11-4-08.....that we could breath a sigh of
relief....we had been cheated out of the past two elections....with
many believing that Bush was never legally elected president of
the United States....and we were braced for the worst.......this can,
and MUST be fixed before 2012, so that this never happens again,
and in the interest of all who support fair and open elections--
regardless of party. Accordingly, it is urged that we adopt the
following proposed "FAIL-SAFE ELECTRONIC VOTING ACT":

THE FAIL-SAFE ELECTRONIC VOTING ACT

1) EVERY electronic voting machine (hereafter EVM), must be
inexpensive, identical throughout the U.S. in a 1/150 ratio, and
must count and produce a hard-copy of the recorded votes. In
addition, an extra copy of their recorded votes would be produced
(not necessarily a hard-copy), marked "Voter's Copy", and
containing "NOTICE: Do Not Destroy Until Every Election On
Your Ballot Is Certified". [If Wal-Mart refused to give us a receipt

for our purchases—would they not be suspect—and this regards our democracy].

2) *After confirming that their votes are recorded correctly*, the voter would then insert the hard-copy ballot into a software-free (count only) optical scanner (hereafter OS), for a second count. The hard-copy ballot would be retained by election officials in the event a candidate asks for a recount (*not possible under the current system, and which undermines the legality of each such election*). The EVM and the OS must be manufactured by different companies (which is universally true today).

3) Election officials assigned to oversee the EVM, would be prevented by law from overseeing the OS, and vice-versa, and stiff criminal penalties would be imposed for violations.

4) Further, every EVM would be programmed with raw data re the total registration rolls, by party, and norms for their voting history, etc.,----as an "alert" to a possible irregularity, such as an "Under-vote"—or "vote-flipping" etc., and *standards* established to suspend certification where there is an "improbable result", at least temporarily, of a particular election until the discrepancy is cleared up. (This is what computers do best, and it would be very easy to create such a program).

5) At the end of the election day, tallies would be taken from the

EVM and the OS, for each candidate. *If the tallies didn't balance for any given election, or if there is an "alert", that election cannot be certified until the "error" is corrected.* If the candidates agree (the victory is certain), minor discrepancies in the count could be disregarded. While probably rare, the Voter, or a random sample of Voters, would be required by law to return their Copy of the recorded votes to the election office to clear up any "error", or where an "alert" signals the need for same.

6) Further, every state provides for a recount when the total vote falls below a certain percent of difference between the candidates, impossible to conduct with the current EVM—and thus Congress must mandate the following regarding presidential candidates: A RUN-OFF election is mandated and triggered in those states where the percent of total vote is less than .5% of difference between any given candidates; said election to be held on the second Saturday following the election, on PAPER BALLOTS ONLY, and contain ONLY the names of the relevant candidates, for instance: "Barack Obama, Democrat" and "John McCain, Republican"—with oversight in counting by a representative(s) of each party—said procedure providing more than adequate time to meet the Electoral College mandate. NOTE: Had this been the law in 2000, Al Gore would be our president, and the American economy would not be in meltdown!

7) Finally, absent the above safeguards, and until these safeguards are in place--Congress must mandate that PAPER BALLOTS, ONLY, can be used in our presidential elections. This is not a "partisan" issue, it is a "pro-democracy" issue. Most importantly, this will return the responsibility for our elections, and our vote counting, back into the hands of the individual voter, where it belongs, and out of the hands of "corporate control"---*it is after all "our democracy", itself, that is at risk if we don't take these steps---and in that regard, is there any time or cost differential that is too great?*

Reply To: Jim Green -- Democrat candidate for Congress, Dist 21, TX, 2000

jgreen5@satx.rr.com   www.Inclusivism.org

CHAPTER SEVEN

Editor/NY Times:

The Republican strategy in this election—the same as with
President Truman in 1948—is to speak of President Obama as if
he is a person who doesn't know how to tie his own shoes—
hmmmm...

For the 18% who will not vote for Romney because he is Mormon,
the 16% of women who favor President Obama over
Romney/Ryan—and 0% of blacks who will vote for R/R—this
strategy is obviously not working—

Integral to this strategy, however, is a wanton disregard for FACTS
[by their own statement], and the TRUTH—indeed, possibly the
most egregious in American history—but consistent with the
Republican strategy to lie, cheat and rob to get elected—so they
can again lie, cheat and rob America blind, if elected!

But we need to drill down on that faction in America, many closet
racists, who are indifferent to this specious Republican strategy—
and to whom this strategy is directed—

For instance, yesterday, at the doctor's office, I engaged a fellow senior about the election [us older, white guys all have an opinion—on everything]—

But he wanted to give me $5 to go see the "birther" movie "2016" [apparently believing that I needed to be "informed"]—and when I informed him that this was a propaganda film [the same strategy Hitler used]—and that it was riddled with lies [and totally disregards, or is ignorant of the fact that "Hawaii is a STATE"]—

He told me that he didn't care "if the movie is riddled with LIES"1

Whoa, folks—this is new, and it is dangerous--we are into a whole new gear, here, folks, and perhaps this is what distinguishes this from every previous election in American history!

A democracy will only work by our having an "informed" electorate—we cannot make accurate decisions—without accurate facts--but when we have a faction of our electorate who don't care if Romney and Ryan are lying [if Ryan's lips are moving....]—or that propaganda put out by the Republican Party is false-----this means America is headed for a world of hurt—picture this—if the engineers lied regarding the data in our moon landing would we Americans have accomplished this amazing feat?

The odds makers give President Obama a 75% chance of winning—but with the fraudulent "vote fraud" legislation in our battleground states, and the manipulation of our flawed electronic voting system—and President Obama is cheated out of this election—

It is US, the American people, and an America based on a foundation of fraud and lies—that will be forced to suffer the consequences! HINT: If you don't care if R/R are liars—Do AMERICA a favor and DON'T VOTE!

Jim Green, Democrat candidate for Congress, 2000 [See also: "Why President Obama Lost The 2012 Election" on Amazon/Kindle]

CHAPTER EIGHT

Editor/NYTimes:

There is a wise and trusted adage "Don't change horses in the middle of the stream" and never has it had more relevance than in this election—

As we are all aware, except for those who are comatose—our economy was in a major meltdown when President Obama took office—we were losing 700,000 jobs a month—and 2.8 million jobs had already been lost in 2008—with the rate of loss matched only with the Great Depression--

The situation demanded action—NOW!

The lesson from the Great Depression has an interesting medical metaphor—and ironically, we discovered our error somewhat in the same time-frame. Prior to the 30's conventional medical wisdom held that the way to treat "shock" was by cutting off the blood supply—and not infrequently the patient died—

In response to the collapse of the market in 1929, it was the conclusion of the FED to cut off the money supply—which, as we all know now, drove the economy straight over a cliff—and prolonged the Depression by at least 10 years!

The lesson learned in medicine in the treatment of "shock" was to increase the blood supply, not cut it—and for our economy, every credible economist since agree that to fix our economy we need to infuse it with cash—and plenty of it!

Fast forward to today. It is interesting the selective memory loss on the part of Republicans regarding our "Stimulus Bill"—No, not the one by President Obama—but rather the one by President Bush on February 8, 2008 [where was the Tea Party, then?]— when the storm clouds posed an ominous economic future—and then the $700 billion TARP signed by President Bush, later in 2008—

But when President Obama's Stimulus Bill came along in February, 2009 [on the advice of every credible economist in America, on the right or left]—and a third in tax cuts—the Republican propaganda machine went into high gear to paint him as a "tax and spend" liberal—The lying SOB's—And the lie continues to this day!

Jim Green, Democrat candidate for Congress, 2000

CHAPTER NINE

EDITOR/NYTimes:

RE DEBATES: WHERE IS THE ROMNEY APOLOGY?

James Baker, former Treasury Secretary under President Reagan, wildly praised President Obama on Fareed Zakaria's GPS, in early 2009—for using the "Stimulus" to put a floor under our economy in meltdown—

The reason: Because Baker did the EXACT same thing in 1987—following Black Monday, October 19, 1987—when the Market lost a quarter of its value in one day and our economic experts were predicting another Great Depression...

So where was the Tea Party then—blathering on about Reagan/Baker being "tax and spend" liberals? —[The Romney/Ryan "cheap shot" being taken at President Obama—and devoid of decency]—And to this day virtually every "rank and file" Republican believes that President Obama is a wild "tax and spend" liberal—as a result of the "Stimulus"—Absent an APOLOGY!

It is obvious that President Obama would have vastly preferred spending the $6 trillion making America energy independent and on developing alternative fuel sources—

But as both Treasury Secretaries, Baker and Geithner, fully understood—the "Stimulus" was the lesson from the Great Depression—when the FED erroneously cut off the money supply, then, and prolonged the Great Depression by 10 years!

The "Stimulus" was the ONLY doctor in Town—and what has not been said by anyone—if McCain had won he would have spent the same $6 trillion [maybe more]—because that would have been the advice of every credible economist in America—on the right or left!

The fact is, Reaganomics—which Romney promises to return to, if elected—has a shelf-life of 7 years before the economy collapses under the weight of the false premise upon which it is based!

We cannot siphon America's wealth away from the consuming middle and add the short-fall in revenue created by obscene tax cuts to the 1%, to the deficit [Reaganomics by definition]— without driving our deficit through the overheads, exploding our unemployment, and driving our economy over a cliff!

Our deficit was only $60 billion, in 1980—as a result of inept and corrupt Reaganomics—the Republicans ran our deficit to a criminal $10 trillion by 2008—and the above was the result!

And Romney should not be permitted to say another word in this election, or in the Presidential Debates—until he profusely apologizes to the American people for the DAMAGE Republican policies did to America—as a matter of DECENCY!

Jim Green, Democrat candidate for Congress, 2000 [See also: "My Letters To President Obama" on Amazon/Kindle]

CHAPTER TEN

MEMO: Economic Policy Institute

The missing component in our job creation solutions is "the human need to work and be a productive human being"—and evident in the statement that "anybody willing to work should be able to find a job".

Had this been factored into our "mind-set" about how to fix our unemployment crisis—our approach, and the outcome, would have been totally different.

Unfortunately, however, Republicans and Democrats—[our conventional 'wisdom'] is still laboring under the myth, advocated by conservatives, that "humans are lazy and don't want to work"—and evident by our celebrating "Welfare-To-Work" [to get those lazy bums off the dole]—an egregious insult to human integrity, and to the true nature of man!

In short, we should be holding our head in shame regarding this ugly insult—most on welfare would have much preferred to have been working all along, but people cannot apply for jobs that don't exist—[the point most missed—and needed to be fixed]--

and we are now paying the price—THAT WE GOT IT WRONG—
failed to factor in "the human need to work and be a productive
human being"— 1

And, Our 8.1% unemployment rate is consummate proof—

Jim Green, Democrat candidate for Congress, 2000

CHAPTER ELEVEN

POSTED ON FACEBOOK.

The FRAUD in the bogus voter ID laws invented by radical Republicans at ALEC—are the laws themselves—i.e., where is our federal law making it illegal to perpetrate this FRAUD on the American people to suppress the vote—in violation of the Voting Rights Act--with fines/imprisonment for anyone perpetuating this FRAUD? Jim Green, Democrat candidate for Congress, 2000

CHAPTER TWELVE

President Obama/Fellow Democrats.

Kansas is my home state [currently live in Texas]—hometown El Dorado--

Following the 2010 election, the Republican-controlled Kansas legislature passed a voter ID law [part of the behind closed door scam perpetrated on the American people by ALEC—and cropping up in Republican-controlled statehouses all across America since the 2010 election—albeit, not news to the informed].

The following is a personal experience with this law—and the criminal suppression of the vote--

In a conversation with my older brother [a retired attorney], yesterday—and a life-long Democrat—he was told that he would need a new photo for his ID—which could only be taken with a particular camera—but when he asked to have his picture taken—was told the camera was broken!

My brother is 88, he was a former U.S. Attorney under President Kennedy!

If he is prevented from voting—how far reaching can this criminal suppression of the vote extend?

Our democracy is under siege on two fronts in this election, fellow Democrats—and we need to create federal legislation making both illegal—declaring them to be unconstitutional— [and while having zero chance of passing the House—the legislation would create public awareness and act as a warning to the electorate].

1] Declare Citizens United to be unconstitutional [it put America up for sale to the highest bidder] and reinstate contribution restrictions to a pre-Citizens United status [or better, mandate public financing of our elections].

2] Make it unlawful to suppress the vote with the fraudulent claim of "voter fraud"—when there is virtually no evidence of same—and make it a crime punishable by fine/imprisonment to suppress the vote by perpetuating this fraud. In the balancing of interests—the right to vote is infinitely greater.

Finally, it would also be ideal if we could limit the Republicans to not more than one lie on any given day—in their "Big Lie" strategy to steal the presidency—except that Ryan would be arrested before breakfast—

But levity aside, fellow Democrats, we have a crisis on our hands—and while the above may not be acceptable—we have a constitutional imperative on our hands and we can't stand idly by and just let it happen....IMHO

Jim Green, Democrat candidate for Congress, 2000 –See also: "OUR GREED & IGNORANCE: Poses A Far Greater Threat To America, Than Terrorism" on Amazon/Kindle

CHAPTER FOURTEEN

Editor/NYTimes:

For the better part of the past 20 years I have corresponded with a professor at Rutgers University—and a few years back we got into a protracted discussion regarding the definition of "self-esteem".

I don't think we can overestimate the relevance and impact of this concept on our elections.

The discussion started when a study " The Dark Side of High Self-Esteem" reported that criminals have "high self-esteem".

I've seen a few flawed studies—but this took the cake—i.e., the premise is patently absurd—and the "researchers" had confused "high self-esteem" with "arrogance"—I argued, and this is where the discussion started—

To drill down abit—I asked if Hitler was a person with "high self-esteem"—his answer is at the conclusion—

Our discussion explored two opposing points of view—one, "internal"—the other "external". The "internal" is based on an internal sense of one's own sense of self-worth—irrelevant to external factors [the definition of high self-esteem I adhere to].

While "external" regards a person basing their "self-esteem"—
their self worth on props they surround themselves with—such as
a house, or car—or on a more personal level—their looks, or a
good head of hair.

Problem is, given the vagaries of life we can lose our external
props—and we get old--and can lose our hair.

With the lesson being that creating our sense of self worth on the
latter…on external factors, is ephemeral—not an accurate
measure of, or a correct definition of "high self-esteem".

The over-arching point of this discourse is the belief [and I am
certain that I am correct, on this] that we have an epidemic of
"low self-esteem" in America—our angry, old white guys who
vote Republican—as an external prop to bolster their feelings of
low self-esteem—to make themselves feel important—and it is
destroying America!

Data shows that 50% of these pathetic souls have the delusion
that they will be millionaires someday—and they vote
Republican—so they will be prepared—even though they may
not have a pot to piss in—and are voting against the economic
interests of their children! It is the premise of "What's The Matter
With Kansas"

We cannot over-estimate the danger these loonies pose to America—

Jim Green, Democrat candidate for Congress, 2000

CHAPTER FIFTEEN

Editor/NYTimes:

Folks---We need to pull back the curtain and look at what is really behind the Republican agenda in this election.

First, we have tiny, tiny, tiny handful of Americans who are willing to chip in over a billion dollars to get Romney/Ryan elected—

And we need to drill down on who these folks are, and ask what do they want? For one, these are business people—they are not going to gamble that kind of cash unless they plan on getting a payoff for their gamble—

And their payoff, folks, is to have their taxes cut even further—so they can turn their billion dollars, into two billion—and not just via the tax cuts but also by hiding their cash in tax sheltered accounts in the Cayman Islands, etc., rather than investing in America, ad nauseam!

In short, folks—if this tiny, tiny, tiny handful [the 1%] is chipping in over a billion dollars to get Romney/Ryan elected--the last candidates us 99% should be voting for—is Romney/Ryan!

Jim Green, Democrat candidate for Congress, 2000

CHAPTER SIXTEEN

Editor/NY Times

There will be a lot of "buyer's remorse" on the part of rank and file Republicans—who voted for Romney/Ryan—if they should actually win—

They will be like the guy who woke up from a serious hangover and found out he had thrown the family cat through the neighbor's window [an old Shelley Berman joke]—

Most of the rank and file I have talked to are so blindly zealous in their vote "against" President Obama—[some based on racism]-- they don't have a clue what Romney/Ryan has in store for them.

Specifically, to pick up right where Bush II left off—and we all know how that turned out! Been there—did that—it is called "Supply-Side" or "Reaganomics"—IT DOESN'T WORK! IT IS WHAT CAUSED THE GREAT RECESSION IN 2008!

The national Republican Party has but a single agenda—TO PANDER TO THE GREED OF THEIR WEALTHIEST CONTRIBUTORS! Period! That's it—and rather than investing in the betterment of America, they hide their wealth in secret bank accounts to avoid investing in America--!

Further, we can't siphon America's wealth away from the consuming middle, and give it to the already wealthy, without sending our economy into a tailspin!

"Supply-Side" has a shelf-life of about 7 years before the false premise upon which it is based starts caving in on itself—as we learned in our economic collapse in 1987 and again in 2008 [and getting worse each salvo from this corrupt scheme]—and it has cost the American taxpayers trillions of dollars to put a floor under our economy, in the inevitable meltdown!

President Obama had the grim task, from his first day in office, of saving America from another Great Depression, in 2009—

And the Republican propaganda machine has the gall to snow the rank and file with the false blather [flat out lie] that Obama was a "tax and spend" liberal—Obama is a moderate CONSERVATIVE! And if McCain had been elected he would have taken the exact same steps—the choice was "Stimulus" or an ultra-severe Depression—Period! We were losing 700,000 jobs a month!

Finally, the starting point in our political discussion in this election—MUST begin with a Republican apology as assurance to the American people they will not return to the same failed policies that almost sunk America!

So what rank and file Republicans should be asking, now, is where is the Romney/Ryan profuse apology to the American people for the damage Republican policies have done to America?

Jim Green, Democrat candidate for Congress, 2000 See also: My Letters To President Obama, on Amazon/Kindle

CHAPTER SEVENTEEN

Letter to editor/NY Times:

Doesn't it strike anyone as odd that Paul Ryan rails, daily, over deficits under President Obama—indeed, holding himself out, now, as a champion of deficit reduction—WHEN he voted to drive up our deficit by over $5 trillion, while in Congress, under Bush II!

Actually, "odd" may be too kind—maybe "disingenuous" [which is the polite way to say someone is a lying SOB]—"Aw shucks" , Ryan is a lying hypocrite—it is the only honest description that fits!

And to add insult to injury, Ryan now wants to decimate [i.e., destroy] Medicare—[read Ryan's Budget]--so he can give the money saved to the Republican's wealthiest contributors—their payoff for getting him elected! What a guy!

We won't even go to his Draconian approach regarding "women's rights", [including being anti-choice]—and evident by his co-sponsoring legislation with Akin, Ad Nauseam!

And he is doing all of this while claiming to be a "Christian" [actually Catholic]—seems he has forgotten that if one is not following the teachings of Christ, one is NOT a Christian! Which the "Nuns On A Bus" have been quick to remind him!

And if the reader does not know that the sole agenda of the National Republican Party, the same as Ryan, is to make the rich, richer—and them poorer—they are not paying attention!

But getting back to the deficit, please consider this metaphor, If one of our children spills a glass of milk—we wipe it up with some paper towels—but if they spill a whole gallon—we grab a mop and a bucket and everything else at hand to clean up the mess—

And, President Obama was handed a mega-spill to clean up— from day one—as a direct result of the mess caused by Ryan, and the rest of the Republicans over the past 8 years!

In short, it cost us—the American taxpayers $4 trillion just to clean up the $10 trillion mess left by the Republicans, i.e., it was this "mop and bucket" President Obama had to use to prevent another Great Depression!

Finally, you would think Romney and company would, first, profusely apologize to the American people for the mess they left—and then promise never to pull this gimmick on the American people again--

But they have the gall to tell us they are going to double-down—
i.e., pick up right where Bush II left off!

Do they think we are stupid? Don't answer that....

Jim Green, Democrat candidate for Congress, 2000

ANTHOLOGY IV

WHY PRESIDENT OBAMA LOST THE 2012 ELECTION: A Wake-
Up Call

PROLOGUE:

The 2012 election has yet to take place as I write—but if
President Obama does lose, I will be one of the most
disappointed—

Not only because I am a cheerleader—but also because it will
mean that America is finished!

After being plundered when the Republicans have held the White
House over the past 30 years, America cannot handle another
round of Republican's "lie, cheat, and rob" to get elected, so they
can "lie, cheat and rob" America blind—once elected!

Indeed, Romeny, Limbaugh, Bockmann, Ryan, etc., —the gang—
have sanctioned a level of lying unheard of in prior elections--To
borrow from Gore Vidal—"Lying to someone who is dying, by
saying they look good, is good manners—but lying to get elected
is dangerous"—and for the current crop of Republicans--if their
lips are moving, they are lying!

And, it is time for Americans to start identifying these persons for what they are—"Not Decent People"—[decent people would never do what they are doing]--And as we add MD to the end of a medical doctor's name--we need to henceforth add NDP to the name of every Republican to whom this applies—starting with the "gang", above....for instance, Paul Ryan, NDP....and the GOP has been traded for NDP....

And the Akin debacle in Missouri [Akin and Ryan co-sponsored "personhood" legislation, even if it was the result of rape—which their legislation re-defined to minimize]—and which underscores in red just how far the Republican Party has fallen into this abyss, which rebukes modernity, science and critical thinking! The Republican Party has sold its soul in their desperation to pursue the anti-Christian agenda—of GREED, just for the sake of GREED--and forgotten the adage "Lay down with dogs, and get up with fleas" [and no apology regarding the definition of anti-Christian hypocrites—if one is not following the teachings of Christ—they are NOT a Christian]!

Regarding our unemployment crisis, Howard Schultz, CEO of Starbucks, makes a great cup of coffee—but he doesn't know beans [no pun intended] about how to fix our unemployment crisis—and this is cited because Mr. Schultz, and with every good intention, started "Create Jobs for USA". Problem is, he is still looking to the market to solve this problem....The dilemma for the business community is that while every waking moment in capitalism is spent pondering how to eliminate as many of us humans, as possible, from the workplace—to increase profits—what can't be ignored is the Halo effect high unemployment has on consumer confidence--people stop buying the products made by the business community--when we have high unemployment....

Thus, the bottom line is, and a major question asked in this book—HOW DO WE FIX OUR UNEMPLOYMENT CRISIS?

And, in part, the purpose of this book is to provide the answer.

Writing this book as a post-mortem, however, is a vehicle to look at issues from the perspective of "hindsight is 20-20" —and as Oscar Wilde averred "The only truly worthless opinion, is an unbiased one."—so what you will read, here, is my analysis of how we got where we are—and what we need to do to solve our problems in a 21st Century world—

Finally, here—I published my first book on my 78th birthday—and I have published one a month, on average, since [this is the 5th]—not that I write that fast, or well—they are all compilations of writings gathering dust over the past 30 years—and with a growing outrage how we are becoming a plutocracy or oligarchy, take your pick—

And to protect this tiny handful of rulers [and while claiming to be the most free country on earth]—we have had an explosion in prison building over this 30 years—passing up every other nation on earth in prison population by 1990, and we now have more Americans in prison than any other civilized country in the world—we have the same prison population as China—But they have a billion more people! Specifically, we now have 5% of the world's population, and 25% of all prison inmates on earth in our prisons!

And this is due in large part because we [Republicans and Democrats, alike—albeit, Republicans by far the worst offender] are unwilling or unable to create programs that will solve our unemployment crisis!

Yes, we have NO job creation program in America—real job creation, either proposed [except HR 870]--or on the books!

That is, we have never looked at unemployment as a "stand alone" social problem—but rather it is seen as a step-child to market recovery—i.e., if the market fails, the unemployed are out of luck! More on this shortly—

Finally, a note to the reader—if you are a "typo-wonk"—are more concerned with sentence structure, etc., than content—you probably won't like my writing—and a wayward capital letter, here and there, and appearing out of place and used for emphasis—editorial license—so apologies, here—just look for content, please....THX

Chapter One

THE HISTORY OF HOW WE GOT WHERE WE ARE.

In the mid-1970's, the colliding forces of automation, technology, globalization, etc., reached a critical mass, resulting in ubiquitous unemployment in all of the OECD countries, and has left their leaders conflicted, ever since, regarding the displaced employee— Eurozone unemployment is still in double digits, with Spain at 22.9%, and with high youth unemployment a major factor in Arab Spring.

In the U.S., we took a pro-active role in addressing, and as a direct response to this economic shift—and in 1978 President Carter signed into law 15 USC § 3101--which "authorizes" the creation of a "reservoir of public employment" at any time our unemployment in America exceeds "3%".

The following year, in 1979, however, and in a panic over Humphrey-Hawkins—our ultra-conservative foundations, and desperate to preserve the "market only" job creation concept, embraced a flawed paper by an obscure MIT student, David L. Birch "The Job Generation Process"; and [with lots of cash] gave his paper biblical importance, and every president since has cited his finding as gospel.

Birch's paper concluded that "small businesses" were the greatest generator of new jobs—problem is, for the purposes of policy-making—it is BS. In a study at Harvard University in 2010, "The Myth of Small Business Job Creation" The research shows "no systematic relationship between firm size and growth." And that small businesses can actually detract from job growth—nevertheless, it is still the Republican One and Only job creation solution!

And in spite of this Washington struggles, still, to make this antiquated and unworkable notion, work--that it is only the market that can create jobs—the world has changed, our solutions haven't, and the result has been a disaster, politically as well as otherwise!

It would be impossible to still have 8.3% unemployment if we were on the right path [the result is the proof]—and among other problems with this concept--if the market fails, the unemployed are out of luck [It is the reason Romeny's job creation solution is a farce!].

Further, unemployment is a "social" problem we are seeking to address with a highly unstable, incompatible entity. The Market --That is, the last place we should look for a reliable solution to our unemployment crisis is The Market....

And, what apparently isn't clear going forward in the 21st Century, is that an expanding and contracting public workforce is an INDISPENSABLE component to the correct functioning of a modern market economy—i.e., The Humphrey-Hawkins Full Employment Act was dead-on correct in 1978—and provided a "win-win" solution for America--

The market thrives when we have a robust, employed, consuming workforce, and it is essential to consumer confidence—and overlooked is that HR 870 [currently in Committee], and the proposed "Neighbor-To-Neighbor Job Creation Act" [hereafter NTN] See: www.Inclusivism.org [both authorized under Humphrey-Hawkins], are deficit-neutral--Pro-Market "win-win" solutions. The American people win, and capitalism wins—

Chapter Two

THE MYTHS AND GOBLINS THAT HINDER OUR PROGRESS

The damage caused by our high unemployment is almost incalculable—for the business community as well as the unemployed--and it would be impossible to have 8.3% [almost one in 10 Americans] unemployed—if we were on the right path to fix this extremely serious social/economic/political problem—

And the problem, in large part, is because unemployment is _not_ addressed as a stand-alone "social" problem—but rather, is seen as a step-child to market recovery—and the obvious downside to this mind-set--if the market fails, the unemployed are out of luck!

Former editor of the Harvard Business Review, Dr. David Ewing, in his book "Freedom Inside The Organization" [1977] observed "Employee rights are like a black hole in space, so impacted by tradition that light can barely escape.".

And it is these "traditions" [and loaded with myths] that we need to drill down on so that we can both analyze why we are where we are—and also so we can bring our "job creation" into the 21st Century.

For instance, the panic by the untra-right foundations in 1979, noted above, and their desperate efforts to undermine Humphrey-Hawkins is from the deeply held belief and tradition that the American "employee" is to be drawn from "a pool of slaves" to be used and discarded "at will".

In short, they still have one foot firmly planted on the plantation....

And this also explains their systematic destruction of unions in America, and the millions they have spent enacting "Right To Work" laws in 24 of our 50 states [the title of these laws a joke, of course]—because they have nothing to do with the "right to work", but rather the elimination of unions in these states—so that "employees" can be drawn from a pool of slaves to be used and discarded "at will"....

In short, we have a very steep hill to climb to bring us into the 21st Century—and particularly when we have tens of millions of dollars being spent to keep us on the plantation...

Another irony in the misnomer "Right To Work" states--when we superimpose the map over the "red vs blue" states the match is eerily similar—Those states with Right To Work laws are almost all red, and vice-versa.

Also compounding this is a lack of understanding [having the wool being pulled over their eyes]--on the part of a gullible public, to use an environment metaphor.

It is transparent why our "profiteers" want to eliminate the EPA, and driven by pure GREED—so they can drill the Rocky Mountains down to an ant hill—but the "rank and file" support this plunder of our earth for a single reason. Jobs

That is, persons who by all that is right should not be anti-environment—Are so immersed in the tradition that jobs can only be created by the Market, i.e., the belief that they wouldn't be able to get a job unless we go along with this plunder—so they too, would destroy the planet for a "good paying job"—a tragic dilemma for mother Earth, and us inhabitants!

Another irony, is that "most [Americans think] that anybody willing to work should be able to find a job" a quote from the "The Audacity of Hope" –the quote goes on to add "that paid a living wage."—but this is a given, and not that the minimum wage laws are the answer but they protect against exploitation.

What is most interesting about this quote, however, is that we are a democracy and if most Americans believe that "anybody willing to work should be able to find a job" [86% according to a recent Zogby poll]—where are our laws to make it a reality?

In short, the American people are saying fix unemployment, and this will in turn fix the economy—rather than the other way around—a point not lost on the "occupy" movement....

And, under the "authorization" in Humphrey-Hawkins at no time should our unemployment in America exceed "3%".

To understand why our unemployment is not now at 3%, we need to drill down on our solutions being "so impacted by tradition that light can barely escape.".

For instance, and to dissect two separate interviews:

On GPS, on January 29, 2012, Timothy Geithner stated in response to the question from Fareed Zarkaria, when we could expect jobs to return, Mr. Geithner strapped the solution to our unemployment crisis to "How fast we grow", i.e., how fast the market [our economy] grows—AND, in an interview on CNN of August 3, 2012, and in response to the same question, Austan Goolsbee responded "Jobs are tied to the economy".

The responses are linked together because they are both saying the same thing—their responses are coming from the same mind-set.

Mr. Geithner and Mr. Goolsbee, are our brightest and best—they went to our best schools--Mr. Geithner is the current United States Secretary of the Treasury, Mr. Goolsbee is former Chairman of the Council of Economic Advisers to President Obama.

In neither interview did the respondents say I am very sorry to say that our only means to create jobs in America is via market recovery—because both believe that our current methodology is correct—i.e., our hands a tied and current economic theory will not allow us to think outside the "conventional wisdom" box—

That is, in looking at unemployment as a stand-alone "social" problem—that MUST be solved independent of, and separate from the market—but this is not even on the table, indeed, even on the radar—neither of these gentlemen, however, are ill-willed, or ill-intentioned—they are just wrong....

Mostly, they don't understand the problem they have been asked to solve—for instance, if the federal government [the CDC] took the same approach in the AIDS crisis—as the federal government, to date, has taken in solving our unemployment crisis—we would still have tens of thousands dying from this dread disease!

And anyone believing that the Republicans, and particularly Romney, thinks any differently, or even has a clue--is from another planet! Indeed, Romney believes this archaic mind-set is the word of God!

In short, this antiquated mind-set is "conventional wisdom" in America—and it is why we have 25 million Americans unemployed, or underemployed! And lest we forget— "conventional wisdom" once held that the world was flat—[and world travel was out of the question]....and it needs to be challenged, in this instance—BECAUSE IT DOESN'T WORK! The result is the proof....

The really sad conclusion to this chapter, however, is that had the Democrats [when they had the opportunity], in fact, given "job creation" the social/economic/political importance it should have had—and reduced unemployment to 3%--the Tea Party would be meeting in a phone booth--the 2010 election would not have been a disaster--and all the good work of the Obama administration would have been Bulletproof, rather than as it has turned out. A Target

Chapter Three

WHAT WE NEED TO DO GOING FORWARD IN THE 21ST CENTURY.

Inexplicably "public employment" is seen the same as WPA—where millions are employed directly by the federal government—when that model is not only outmoded—it is insufficient to address our problems in the 21st century.

What we need today is an expanding and contracting public workforce—that expands during downturns in the market, and contracts as employees return to the private sector [Google: The Buffer Stock Employment Model]—triggered anytime our unemployment exceeds "3%" [as "authorized" under Humphrey-Hawkins]--and least understood. This is an INDISPENSABLE component in the effective functioning of our 21st Century Market.

The market thrives when we have a robust, employed, consuming workforce—our manufacturers are sitting on $2 trillion in cash because they do not have consumers for their products—i.e., absent consumers, they lay off employees—[and the Republican solution, Reaganomics, has acted as an accelerate to this downward spiral—and which Romney promises to return us to if he is elected]¡

In short, the above model is a "win-win" solution—the American people win, and capitalism wins!

To achieve this, what is being urged is "The Neighbor-To-Neighbor Job Creation Act"¡ A federally mandated, mutual insurance—owned by our employed [from janitor to CEO] to create a fund to hire/train our unemployed.

To be viable, however, our job creation solution *MUST* contain¡

1] Be based on the premise that we have far more work that needs to be done in America, than we have persons to fill these jobs.

2] It MUST have renewable funding.

3] It will not add a dime to our deficit.

To expand briefly, it is currently believed, erroneously, that we need "make work" jobs so that everyone who wants to work will have a job—but this is absurd—and an insult to "Yankee Ingenuity".

We do not have an unemployment crisis from a shortage of jobs, or money—but rather from a shortage of imagination.

Regarding "renewable funding" ALL of our job creation solutions, to date, have been based on the mind-set, "jump start" the market, and the market will in turn create all the jobs we need— and even setting aside that this is untrue, our current job creation is moving at a snail's pace—long past the unemployment benefits drying up—with the CBO projecting that even with the JOBS Act, signed into law on April 6, 2012--it will be 2017 before we return to a barely acceptable 5.5% unemployment rate!

Further, by its nature when we "jump start" --the employment ends when the funding runs out as we learned from the Stimulus—whereas any real fix to our unemployment crisis _demands_ renewable funding....

And whether the electorate will accept an unemployment rate hovering around 8% on election day—is the $64,000 question....

Regarding not adding a dime to our deficit—under The Neighbor-To-Neighbor Job Creation Act [NTN], the _funding_ to reduce our unemployment to 3% comes from an insurance owned by our employed, rather than added to our deficit—

If one is employed in America, participation in this insurance plan is mandatory—similar in concept to our auto insurance or Social Security Insurance [and without question the most successful social program in American history].

Jobs beget jobs--And with a modest policy cost of 4% of salary we can create more "private-sector" jobs in 6 months, that HR 2847, and the JOBS Act, in 6 years—and unlike these laws—NTN will not add a dime to our deficit!

Finally, this is in total concert with the will of the American people, i.e., that "anybody willing to work should be able to find a job"—and the American people have told our politicians time and again of their willingness to chip in to help their neighbor get a job [and as an *insurance* as above, it also protects their continued employment]—it is just that Washington is deaf as an adder!

Chapter Four

THE BLUEPRINT FOR MAKING NTN OPERATIONAL

We have one member of Congress who has a hand on the pulse of the American people, regarding the subject at hand, and is of like-mind with the concept presented, here [albeit his funding is slightly different] —John Conyers from Michigan.

And every Congressional session Representative Conyers introduces an updated version of Humphrey-Hawkins, only to watch it die in Committee—it is currently HR 870, and currently in Committee in the House.

The primary difference between NTN--the proposed, above, and HR 870, is how it is funded—with HR 870 funded with a small fee on transactions on the stock market—i.e., the funding would come from Wall Street. Both, however, address our current 21st Century dilemma--that the world has changed, our solutions haven't, and the result has been a disaster....

The following is the blueprint for implementation of The Neighbor-To-Neighbor Job Creation Act.

1] The Department of Labor would create a National Trust Fund, with funds to be received from existing FICA accounts, and supplemented, if needed, from a windfall profits tax on excessive profits, for instance, by our major oil corporations, etc.

2] A Commission would be set up within the Department of Labor to review grant requests from every jurisdiction in America, including but not limited to states, local governments, Indian tribes, but specifically rejecting "privatization" requests [which historically have cut services to increase profits—and notorious for "cronyism"].

3] The target would be to reduce unemployment to no more than 3% nationally within one year of enactment, i.e., to not more than 3% for persons 20, or over, and not more than 4% for persons 16 or over—and as currently authorized under the Humphrey-Hawkins Full Employment Act [15 USC § 3101]

4] Further, grant funds would be distributed to authorized jurisdictions to train persons for gainful employment.

5] The funding of projects would be bifurcated, i.e., identified as a "national" or "local" project—with national projects, for example, a high-speed rail system, space exploration, alternative energy projects—[Today half of the world's population lives in a megalopolis--"In 1950, there was only one city with a population of more than 10 million—New York City—today, there are 21, and the number of urban areas with populations between five and ten million has shot from 7 to 37." National Geographic, November 2002].

6] Local grant requests could include: Child care for low income families, the urgent need outlined by the NEA for School Modernization, long over-due infrastructure repair, the creation of Federal Regional Diagnostic and Treatment Centers for the diagnosis and treatment of the violent offender—the list of social benefits is almost endless.

7] To the greatest degree possible this Act would be carried out under the over-arching Buffer Stock Employment Model, where public employment would expand during downturns in the market [and triggered at 3% unemployed, as "authorized" under H-H], and contract as employees return to the private sector.

Chapter Five

ECONOMIC INCLUSIVISM. A 21st Century Solution

"There is one thing stronger than all the armies in the world, and that is an idea whose time has come" Victor Hugo

Economic Inclusivism is Neo–Capitalism—Inclusive pro-market solutions to our social problems.

We are in the throes of enormous socio-economic change, and all of the above in this book is a component in a larger, more comprehensive roadmap, I have identified as *Economic Inclusivism*—and which poses the question.

What solutions do we need to apply going forward in a 21st Century world?

It may be too cynical, but many of the solutions today could be compared to pouring gasoline on a fire to put it out....

For one, our insane incarcerate rate—which has made American more dangerous, not less—and undermines the education of our youth; and adding to our deficit with "jump start" job creation—with the jobs ending the minute the funding runs out—and has resulted a cost-effective nightmare....

Our starting point for Economic Inclusivism is based on a truism,
and asserted by every credible economist. "High and persistent
unemployment has pervaded almost every OECD country since
the mid-1970s."— Dr. William F. Mitchell, Economist

So given this reality—what adjustments do we need to make?

Many of our solutions, today, are based on applying the "rules"
that applied prior to this cosmic shift in our economy—but like
"Pouring new wine into old wineskins"—to borrow from
scripture [I'm an agnostic]—the result has been a disaster....

In short, the following bifurcated solutions are devoid of an
ideological agenda—and are based, solely, on being EFFECTIVE
solutions.

Economic Reforms

1] Work must become a legal right. To address our insidious
practice of "exclusion", Congress must enforce a citizen's legal
right to work, as enacted by Congress in "The Full Employment
Act of 1946", and as outlined in the Democratic National Platform
position asserting "Opportunity to every American". We need to

recognize that the right to work and be a productive member of one's society is a human right, as an adjunct to the free enterprise system. Additionally, we need to set in motion the following constitutional amendment, "Work shall hereafter be the legal right of every citizen, and Congress shall, except for retirement/disability programs under federal jurisdiction, make no laws which will abridge the right of any citizen of legal age, to work and be a productive citizen".

2] To ensure enforcement/fund this legal right, Congress would create a federally mandated, mutual insurance--owned by our employed to provide a fund to hire/train our unemployed [outlined in detail, above].

3] Since this program of "inclusion" would address 95% of our social ills (crime, welfare, drugs, etc., and exacerbated in many cases by inept Band-Aid programs), the federal budget could be greatly reduced and our current Federal Income Tax would be replaced with a National Sales Tax, value-added tax, a national lottery, or some combination of taxes other than our current Federal Income Tax. Billions are spent annually trying to get around the Tax Code, all of which is passed on to us, the consumer, in the higher cost of consumer goods.

<u>Social/Prison Reforms</u>

4] We need to re-classify all crime in the future as violent or non-violent, and discard the archaic terms felony and misdemeanor. The term "felony" is fixed in the public's mind as "armed and dangerous"—and yet over 70% of our prison inmates are in prison for non-violent offenses [50% are in for drug related offenses]—and if for no other reason this undermines our intelligently addressing the real problem. The violent offender.

5] We need a much greater use of "Shock" Incarceration [a concept I authored in the 1960's]; a greater use of fines and probation [both civil and criminal], in lieu of incarceration, and an expanded menu of sentencing alternatives. Prison should be a last resort, not first, and through the above social re-structuring we will have far less need for incarceration.

6] We need the creation of Federal Regional Diagnostic and Treatment Centers, for the diagnosis and treatment of the violent offender [And given the recent spate of assaults in Aurora and Wisconsin—and the urgent need to restore the ban on assault weapons—how about a ban on the NRA leadership!]....

7] We need to pick-up the lead taken by England, in treating drug addiction as a "medical" rather than a "criminal" problem, so that we can effectively curb drug-related crime, and keep drugs out of the hands of our youth.

8] A universal healthcare system is an indispensable component of a sane society. We are the only major industrial country in the world without universal healthcare—and we pay twice as much, for half the result [only a slight exaggeration] for our healthcare in America—We are ranked 37th in the world in healthcare by the World Health Organization.

Chapter Six

HOW MUCH SHOULD YOU PAY, HOW MUCH SHOULD I PAY?

The raging issue going on in America, today, turns on this single question—and since 1980 we started seeing more and more tax watchdog groups cropping up all over the place—some by persons who would starve to death if others didn't pay theirs— [Hint: The Tea Party folk]

The driving force behind this demonizing the payment of taxes are the Koch brothers—a slight exaggeration, and slightly unfair—but used here as a metaphor for that tiny, tiny handful, the 400 who now hold more of America's wealth than 50% of the rest of us Americans—and a direct result of their getting Bush II appointed to the presidency!

In fact, a larger question is when does spending billions in propaganda to keep from paying taxes, cease to be cost-effective? And apparently the 1% haven't reached that point yet—but one thing is obvious and that is that their "allegiance is to money", rather than their "allegiance to America"--after all, most got their wealth from us—the 99%--the American people!

And it should be transparent to anyone voting in this election that when these folks want to spend a billion dollars plus to get Romney elected—that the last person us 99% should vote for--is Romney....

The only question we should have on the table in this election is: What kind of America do we want for ourselves? So use your brains, folks—VOTE to re-elect President Obama!

Chapter Seven

FILLING IN THE BLANK SPOTS: Miscellaneous papers and letters

COMMONS SENSE ECONOMICS:

- We cannot siphon America's wealth away from the consuming middle without causing economic collapse—[1987 & 2008— i.e., Supply-Side has a shelf-life of about 7 years]--
- When every waking moment in capitalism is spent pondering ways to eliminate as many of us humans, as possible, from the workplace—to increase profits—why on earth would anyone look to this model to solve an unemployment crisis?
- Unemployment is a "social" problem—and "our government" has an absolute responsibility to step forward with a viable solution.
- We should never condemn the CEO who closes a plant when they are losing money—but we should be outraged by a government that is indifferent or incompetent in finding a viable solution to the resulting "social" problem.
- Capitalism thrives when we have a robust, employed, consuming public—
- "Public-sector" jobs is an accelerate to "private-sector" jobs— and will create more "private-sector" jobs in 6 months, than HR 2847 The HIRE Act, in 6 years, if ever—

- The belief that "public-sector" jobs can only be created by increasing the deficit, or equals a massive government program, such as WPA—is a belief that is suffering from a lack of imagination—
- The Humphrey-Hawkins Full Employment Act which authorizes the creation of a "reservoir of public employees" anytime our unemployment in America rises above "3%" is a Pro-Market solution—and an INDISPENSABLE tool for economic survival in a modern market economy—See also HR 870 [currently in Committee]--
- In the mid-1970's—the colliding forces of automation, globalization, innovation, etc., reached a critical mass, resulting in ubiquitous unemployment—and has left our leaders befuddled with what to do with the displaced employee?
- Our response in America was H-H, above, in 1978—but inexplicably never implemented—and the resulting high unemployment cost Carter the election in 1980--
- "Most [Americans think] that anybody willing to work should be able to find a job." President Obama, "The Audacity of Hope" – it is not the American people standing the in the way our implementing H-H—it is bad advice—
- The correlation between high unemployment and our lethargic economy is absolute—
- A comprehensive public employment program, in compliance with H-H, such a HR 870, or a federally mandated, mutual insurance, owned by America's employed--to hire/train our

unemployed [www.Inclusivism.org]. Is Pro-Market, and pro-
the American people--

Jim Green, Democrat candidate for Congress, 2000

President Obama/Fellow Democrats:

"Conservative" is the big word in Republican parlance in this election—and the candidates stumble all over themselves to say it as many times possible is their 30 second ads--

Indeed, Romney referred to himself as "severely conservative" and even declared that he was "more conservative than Rick Santorum" [which is way out there]—and he went on to say "I'm not concerned about the very poor".

But in drilling down on this a bit—the Republican candidates are obviously trying to appeal to persons who embrace being "conservative"—but what does this mean?

There are different ways to be conservative—a person can be fiscally conservative, and be socially "liberal", or vice-versa—but you get the sense that "severely conservative" is code for I'm not a "liberal".

And after years of Republicans demonizing the word "liberal" in their propaganda ads--it is little wonder that in their prayers at night their followers thank God they are not a "liberal"—

But those who define themselves as "conservative" might do well to look up the definition of the antonym for the word "liberal"-- "illiberal" in Webster's.

And the real shocker for those who are slaves to the labels, i.e., propaganda buzz words, in this election will be shocked to learn that if they buy car insurance—they are a "socialist"—

Yep folks, our car insurance is based on the same collectivist principle as "socialism"—we pool our money to protect us when fate taps us on the shoulder—

And communism differs only in that it is controlled by a totalitarian state dominated by a single and self-perpetuating political party, which, of course, is also its fatal flaw.

Indeed, it is this flaw that has made the extremes on both the right and the left--fascism and communism, fail. It takes a dictator to hold the government in place—and it is the antithesis of a democracy.

In sum, what we need is a "post-label" election—to cut out the noise so the electorate will actually listen what the candidates are saying.

For instance, when Romney says that he wants to cut taxes for the 1% ever further it is consummate proof that he intends to return to the same failed policies that took America, and our economy straight over a cliff!

Jim Green, Democrat candidate for Congress, 2000

President Obama/Fellow Democrats,

For the past 65 years we have had two parallel paths to address unemployment in America—

To assure employment for the troops returning from WW II, President Truman signed into law The Full Employment Act of 1946—

This was expanded upon in 1978 with the Humphrey-Hawkins Full Employment Act, signed into law by President Carter—

And a 21st Century version of this path to full employment in America, is pending the House, HR 870.

Humphrey-Hawkins best defines this path to addressing unemployment in America, and it "authorizes" our government to create a "reservoir of public employees" anytime our unemployment rises above "3%".

And in spite of the fact that this path to employment has been the law of the land since 1946—and is a Pro-Market solution [more on this shortly]---Washington has lacked the wherewithal to implement this path to employment on behalf of the American people—[a point not lost on the "occupy" movement].

Rather, Washington has taken the alternate parallel path—by insisting that human labor is a "component" in the free enterprise system—[barely distinguishable from the machine the human operates] to be used and discarded "at will"—and the Republican propaganda is that it is an attack upon "freedom" to challenge this concept, but whose "freedom"?

As a result, however, "conventional wisdom" has insisted that it is the market, alone, that can fix our unemployment crisis—the result has been a disaster—

The market thrives when we have a robust, employed, consuming public—and by taking this parallel path—we not only have a staggering 8.1% unemployment, but a struggling recovery as well.

Ironically, following WW II, Australia passed a law very similar to our Full Employment Act of 1946—

Difference is—they actually put it into effect—and over the next 30 years—[until the cold winds of conservatism swept in Reagan and Thatcher, etc.] –the government in Australia saw as a solemn responsibility that "anyone willing to work should be provided with a job" [a quote from the "Audacity of Hope"].

The citizens of Australia still refer to this 30 years as their "Golden Age".

Jim Green, Democrat candidate for Congress, 2000
www.Inclusivism.org

Letter to editor/NY Times:

It is a mystery to me why no one is raising the issue that the billions our corporations make in "profits"—creates, at a minimum, a fiduciary obligation to those who brought them these [in some cases obscene] "profits":

It is US, folks—You and me—the American people—the 99%, if you will--and this also creates a fiduciary obligation for the betterment of society—

But these obligations goes out the window when it comes to the corporate Super Pacs—where a GREEDY few are pouring in millions of the dollars they got from us—not for the betterment of America, or the American people—

But rather for their personal aggrandizement—Greed, just for the sake of greed--and at the expense of the economic well being of the 99%! Further, greed, for the sake of greed is antithetical to Christ's teachings! Indeed, the Republican One and Only program is to pander to the GREED of their wealthiest contributors!

What a double-cross—using our money to stick it to us!

And now with the worst decision from the U.S. Supreme Court since the Dred Scott Decision [which set the stage for our Civil

War]—the "Citizens United" decision—this corporate cash can be given in secret, and in unlimited amounts!

Further, with Romney in his daily rants against President Obama, asserting that President Obama doesn't know "When to send jobs overseas"—how much of that cash is coming for Romeny from Indonesia, or Singapore, or China?

Our elections are now for sale to the highest bidder—and we are subjected to a blizzard of propaganda ads on the internet—written by corporate slugs pretending to be legitimate—and paid for by these Super Pacs [our money]!

Surely, everyone can see through this internet BS, can't they? Don't answer that—

Jim Green

ANTHOLOGY V

THE HARVARD BOYS CLUB

THE HARVARD BOYS CLUB is a true story. It contains several sub-themes, and is the source for Economic Inclusivism—the foundation of this book--but the primary story regards a federal judge, who had been a Hitler Youth, who falsified a court record with the INTENT to deny to a U.S. citizen, rights protected by the U.S. Constitution. Did Hitler undermine our freedoms in America, from his grave? The case was appealed to the U.S. Supreme Court—and regards criminal negligence on the part of government officials in the death of our 6 year old son. The sub-themes relate to the desperate struggle by Republicans to regain control of the White House for the express purpose of controlling judicial appointments, particularly to the U.S. Supreme Court [a fact few Americans are aware of]—It also underscores our need for single-payer health insurance in America—as well as the need for systemic change in America. It also touches upon the proliferation of workplace violence, as depicted in the recently released documentary "Murder By Proxy"-

The following "cartoon", a reprint from THE NEW YORKER, is in the archives of the U.S. Supreme Court, in the case cited, to this day. It was included in a Petition For Rehearing [automatic in the appeal process] when the court declined to grant certiorari—i.e., was indifferent my COMPLAINT FOR FRAUD filed against Federal Judge William W Schwarzer, and indifference to the violation of my protected rights under the U.S. Constitution, which resulted from Schwarzer's fraud!

"Excellent , excellent . A fine blend of truths, half-truth, and blatant falsehoods."

IN THE

Supreme Court of the United States

October Term, 1979

No. 79-1627

JAMES L. GREEN,

Petitioner,

VS.

"Excellent, excellent. A fine blend of truths, half-truths, and blatant falsehoods."

ABOUT THE AUTHOR. I was employed in our Criminal Justice System for a cumulative 20 years as a probation officer, with 5 of those years as a chief probation officer. I authored the concept of "Shock Incarceration" which became law in Kansas in 1970, and then was adopted in numerous jurisdictions in the U.S. and also spread to Europe—it is currently identified in the U.S. as "Boot Camp" [as the means to "shock" the young offender—and a total distortion of my original intent—like many ideas, once released, they take on a life of their own and I have also seen referred to as "Scared Straight" and "A taste of prison"]. I also instigated establishment of the first Court Psychiatric Clinic in the U.S., in conjunction with psychiatrists from the Menninger Foundation, as a chief probation officer. Finally, I was the Democrat candidate for Congress, District 21, TX, 2000. I would most define myself as a Social Ecologist-- [albeit my degree is in Psychology]. My web page is www.Inclusivism.org –which has been on the internet since 1996.

OTHER BOOKS BY THIS AUTHOR ON AMAZON/KINDLE/BN:

- THE HARVARD BOYS CLUB: Hitler's Assault On Our Freedoms From His Grave
- MY LETTERS TO PRESIDENT OBAMA: Confessions Of A Compulsive Letter Writer
- OUR GREED AND IGNORANCE: Poses A Far Greater Threat To America, Than Terrorism
- LETTERS ON STEROIDS: Confessions Of A Compulsive Letter-To-The-Editor Writer
- THE FIRST TIME I HAD SEX: And, The Religious Intolerance Attack On America
- WHY PRESIDENT OBAMA LOST THE 2012 ELECTION: A Wake-Up Call
- AMERICA IS ONE SICK MF: Why Greed-Driven America Went Off The Rails....
- EVERY GIVEN SUNDAY: A Scientific Formula To Predict NFL Games

www.ingramcontent.com/pod-product-compliance
Lightning Source LLC
Chambersburg PA
CBHW071408170526
45165CB00001B/211